Russell Kelso Carter

**Songs of perfect love**

Russell Kelso Carter

**Songs of perfect love**

ISBN/EAN: 9783337265175

Printed in Europe, USA, Canada, Australia, Japan

Cover: Foto ©Thomas Meinert / pixelio.de

More available books at **www.hansebooks.com**

SONGS OF

# PERFECT LOVE.

EDITED BY

Capt. R. Kelso Carter
AND
John R. Sweney, Mus. Doc.

Philadelphia: JOHN J. HOOD, 1018 Arch St.

# PREFACE.

HE who fears cannot always obey the command to "offer unto the Lord the sacrifice of praise continually," for fear will find utterance in apprehension of evil or punishment, because it always springs from condemnation. But love knows no condemnation, for love "beareth all things, believeth all things, hopeth all things, seeketh not her own, and never faileth." Now that stream, "which never faileth," can and will run over in a "sacrifice of praise continually;" and hence it is apparent, that he who would obey this command, must be "made perfect in love."

"Out of the abundance of the heart the mouth speaketh." The church will never become a triumphing church till it becomes a singing church. And of what should we sing so much as of the PERFECT LOVE of God? Not only of that love manifested *to us*, when the "only begotten Son" was freely given for our sins; but of love manifested *in us*, when "evil affections die" the "old man is crucified with Christ," and the Eternal Word is incarnated in our souls,—"the life of Christ brought forth within us," the Triune God, who "is love," filling us with His presence, and giving to us that kingdom which is righteousness, peace, and joy in the Holy Ghost." Let those who know, or would know this joy, join in singing the SONGS OF PERFECT LOVE.

R. KELSO CARTER.
JOHN R. SWENEY.

(2)

# SONGS OF PERFECT LOVE.

**1**

## Just Now Believe.

R. KELSO CARTER.

JNO. R. SWENEY.

1. The Saviour speaks, O, hear him say, Hear him say, hear him say, Come
2. The door of mer - cy o - pens wide, O - pens wide, o - pens wide; The
3. There's pardon now for ev - 'ry sin, Ev - 'ry sin, ev - 'ry sin, And
4. The Spir - it comes in Je - sus' name, Je - sus' name, Je - sus' name, To

*CHORUS.*

un - to me, I am the Way; Come, come to me. Je - sus died to
blood of Je - sus cru - ci - fied Flows now for thee.
per - fect pur - i - ty with - in; Come and be free. *Chorus to last verse.*
give thee now the tongue of flame, Full lib - er - ty. Je - sus died to

set you free; Now he'll give you vic - to - ry; The precious blood was
set me free; Now he gives me vic - to - ry; The precious blood was

shed for thee, Just now be - lieve.
shed for me I do be - lieve.

5 O, do not fear to trust the Lord,
Trust the Lord, trust the Lord,
But come relying on his word;
Christ died for thee.

6 The life of faith is wondrous sweet.
Wondrous sweet, wondrous sweet,
To daily sit at Jesus' feet,
Come, come and see.

Copyright, 1886, by JOHN J. HOOD.

3

# 2

# Perfect Love.

1 Cor. xiii.

R. KELSO CARTER.
Feb. 1884.

1. Lord, I pray thee for a bless - ing, Which thou on - ly canst be - stow:
2. Though I have all oth - er grac - es, Though I speak with tongue aflame;
3. Though I yield my earthly trea - sure, Give my bo - dy to the fire:

Here, my deepest need confess - ing, At thy feet my - self I throw.
Though I sit in heavenly pla - ces, Though I mag - ni - fy thy name;
Though my knowledge has no mea - sure, Though all mysteries I de - sire;

Faith and hope have both been given, But there's one, all else a - bove;
I am but as brass resound - ing, Noth - ing in thy sight I prove,
Though I grasp the sacred sto - ry, And by faith the mountains move;

Hast - en from the highest heav - en, Fill my soul with perfect love!
Till, through faith, by grace abounding, I am perfect - ed in love.
Yet in all I dare not glo - ry, Till I'm filled with perfect love.

REFRAIN.

Per - fect love, my Sav - iour; Fill me now with love.

4

## Perfect Love.—CONCLUDED.

Come, almight-y to de-liv-er, Fill me now with perfect love.

4 Give me love that never faileth,
Love that suffers without moan;
That believeth and prevaileth,
Love that seeketh not her own:
Love that never thinketh evil,
But rejoiceth truth to prove;
Love that fears not man nor devil,—
Give me, give me perfect love!

5 Love that every evil cureth,
Doth not envy, vaunteth not;
Beareth, hopeth, and endureth
All that falleth to my lot.
Faith, and hope, and love abideth,
But there's one, all else above;
Lord, my yearning spirit chideth
For thy greatest gift of love.

## 3    Have Faith in God.    R. KELSO CARTER.

R. K. C.                   Mark xi. 22.                   March, 1885.

1. In happy hours,'Neath sunny skies; When, from sweet flowers Glad perfumes rise;
2. When fears bid hearken, When doubts assail, When tempests darken, And clouds pre-  [vail;

No foes affrighting, When thou hast trod Paths of delighting, Have faith in God!
When o'er some treasure Cold lies the sod, Earth has no pleasure, Have faith in God!

3 'Mid pow'rs infernal—
Sin's flag unfurled—
Death that's eternal,
Flesh and the world,
'Mid threats tremendous
From Satan's rod,
Howe'er stupendous,
Have faith in God!

4 Foes all reproving,—
By grace set free,
Mountains removing
Cast in the sea: [ters,
God's sons and daugh-
Walking dry-shod,—
Pass through the waters,
Have faith in God!

5 O'er death victorious,
Conq'ring the grave;
With Christ–the glorious,
Mighty to save—
Ended life's story,
Through bursting clod,
Sweeping to glory,—
Have-faith in God!

5

# 4   Come unto Me.

CHARLOTTE MURRAY.     JNO. R. SWENEY.

1. Je-sus is waiting to welcome the weary, Worn with the world's fruitless
2. Je-sus is waiting, he standeth and knocketh, Calling in love up - on
3. Will you not come? you need no prepa - ra-tion! Stay not to think, but come
4. Oh! I am yearning to see you unburdened, Death did I suf - fer that

striving for peace, Tired with a night-watch, that knoweth no morning;
each one op - pressed, "Come un'-to me, sin - ner, wea-ry and la - den,
just as you are; Bring nothing with you, for love giv - eth free - ly,
you might be free; Will you not come? and by 'life-con - se - cra - tion

CHORUS.

Sick with the heart-ache that earth cannot ease.
I will refresh you and give you my rest."
Peace, perfect peace, that no sorrow can mar.
Try to win others, and bring them to me."

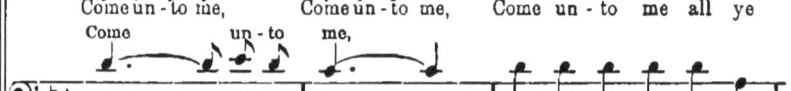

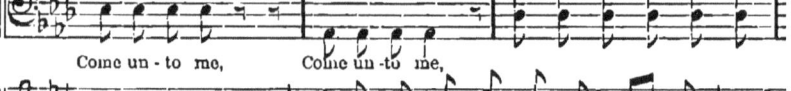

Come un-to me,

Come un-to me,    Come un-to me,

Come un - to me,   Come un-to me,   Come un - to me all ye

Come un - to me,

Come un - to me,   Come un-to me,

wea - ry and la - den, Come un - to me and I'll give you rest.

   6

# 5     Divine Union.

Mrs. MARY D. JAMES.          Mrs. JOSEPH F. KNAPP.

1. Who can un-fold the bliss untold, Dear Saviour, found in thee?
2. To live a-lone for thee—our own Re-deem-er—so a-dored!
3. Oh, hallowed bliss!—no joy like this, Un-fail-ing, sweet, and pure!—
4. Thy ra-diant face, thy matchless grace, Je-sus—thou fair-est One,—

The rapturous love they dai-ly prove Who on-ly Je-sus see.
To do and bear each word and care, For thee, most bles-sed Lord!
Thy love to know in cease-less flow, And feel it will en-dure!
To earth have given the joys of heaven! With thee 'tis heaven be-gun!

CHORUS.

Oh, bles-sed rest! on Je-sus' breast So sweet-ly to re-cline!

Thy voice to hear, so loved, so dear, And know that thou art mine.

By permission.       7       DO RE MI FA SO LA SI

# The Tongue of Praise.

Chas. Wesley.    "My mouth shall show forth thy praise."    R. Kelso Carter.

1. O, for a thousand tongues, to sing My great Redeemer's praise;
2. My gra-cious Mas-ter and my God, As-sist me to pro-claim,
3. Je-sus! the name that charms our fears, That bids our sorrows cease,
4. He breaks the power of canceled sin, He sets the prisoner free;

The glo-ries of my God and King, The triumphs of his grace!
To spread thro' all the earth a-broad The hon-ors of thy name.
'Tis mu-sic in the sin-ner's ears, 'Tis life, and health, and peace.
His blood can make the foul-est clean, His blood availed for me.

REFRAIN.

{ O, glo-ry to God! He breaks the power of sin, Glo-ry to God!
{ O, glo-ry to God! He makes the foulest clean, Glo-ry to God!

He sets the prisoner free; }
His blood avails for me. }

5 He speaks, and, listening to his voice,
  New life the dead receive;
  The mournful, broken hearts rejoice;
  The humble poor believe.

6 Hear him, ye deaf; his praise, ye dumb,
  Your loosened tongues employ;
  Ye blind, behold your Saviour come;
  And leap, ye lame, for joy.

# Coming to Jesus.

Rev. W. H. Burrell.

Jno. R. Sweney.

1. With my sin-wounded soul, To be made ful - ly whole, And thy perfect sal-
2. O, how long have I tried To re - sist nature's tide, All in vain have I
3. I thy promise believe, That in thee I shall live, Thro' thy blood shed so
4. To be thine, wholly thine, Precious Saviour divine; With my all conse-

va-tion to see; With my heart all aglow, To be washed white as snow,
sighed to be free; In myself all undone, 'Neath the waves sinking down,
free - ly for me To ob-tain a pure heart, To secure this "good part,"
crat - ed to thee; To be kept ev'ry hour, By thy love's wondrous power,

REFRAIN.

I am coming, dear Saviour, to thee. I am coming, dear Saviour, to

thee, I am coming, dear Saviour, to thee; With my heart stained by

sin, To be washed and made clean, I am coming, dear Saviour, to thee.

9

DO  RE  MI  FA  SO  LA  SI

# 8   To the World I'm Crucified.

LIZZIE EDWARDS.      JNO. R. SWENEY.

1. Mor-tal tongue can not reveal What a ho-ly joy I feel Since of
2. All my care on him I cast,— I will praise him for the past, And will
3. At the bles-sed mercy - seat, In communion pure and sweet, What a

all a con-se-cration I have made To my Saviour and my King, Whose re-
trust in him whatev-er yet may come; Halle - lu-jah to his name! Ev'ry
brightness from his glory I can see! Oh, how wonderful his grace, That pre-

deeming power I sing, And who once for me was wounded and betrayed.
promise now I claim, Looking upward to my soul's e-ter-nal home.
pares for me a place Where forev-er in his presence I shall be!

*Fine.*

D. S.—world I'm cru-ci-fied, And I know that with my Saviour I shall rise.

**CHORUS.**

Now my troubled heart is stilled, With his fulness I am filled, He is

*D. S.*

holding up the cross before mine eyes; In his love I now a-bide, To the

10

DO RE MI FA SO LA SI

# All to Thee.

R. K. C.

R. Kelso Carter.

1. Je - sus, here I bring my all, Humbly at thy feet I fall,
2. Take my-self, my will, my choice, Means and talent, time and voice,
3. Lead me out to Ol - i - vet, On my brow the thorn-crown set,

In my soul re-solved to prove All that's in re-deeming love.
Loved ones, rep - u - tation's thrall, Present, fu · ture—take it all.
Lean - ing hard, my Lord, on thee, Let me die on Cal - va - ry!

CHORUS.

All to thee, all to thee, Con - se - crat - ed now to thee;

All to thee, all to thee, Let me die, and live in thee!

4 'Neath the judgment-thunders' boom
Lay me in the silent tomb;
Burst the bars, and, cleansed within,
Raise me from the grave of sin.

5 Once for all, myself I give;
Crucified, and yet I live;
Yet not I, but Christ in me
Lives and reigns eternally.

11

# Cast all Thy Care on Me.

LIZZIE EDWARDS.                                         JOHN R. SWENEY.

1. A - mid the changing scenes of time, How dark each life would be With -
2. In ev - ery pang of hu-man woe, In ev - ery throb of pain, His
3. O, who could drink the bit - ter drops That in our cup must fall; Did

out the Sa - viour's lov - ing words, Cast all thy care on me. His
love re - stores a thousand- fold The light of joy a - gain. Though
not the bless'd as - sur - ance come, Our Sa - viour drained them all? And

voice that hushed the rag - ing storm, And calmed the heaving sea, Still
dis - appointments one by one, Our lot on earth must be, The
though the brok - en threads of hope With weep - ing eyes we see, The

whis - pers to the ach - ing heart, Cast all thy care on me.
trust - ing soul looks up to hear, Cast all thy care on me.
same sweet voice our com - fort brings, Cast all thy care on me.

CHORUS.

Cast all thy care on me, cast all thy care on me; Oh,

# Cast all Thy Care on Me.—CONCLUDED.

ten - der, pre - cious, lov - ing words! Cast all thy care on me.

## 11 We Shall Sing.

E. N.

by Per.

1. Soldiers fight - ing in the bat - tle, Up to glo - ry march a-long; Keeping
2. Sing to - day and sing to-morrow, Sing when things are going wrong; Sing the
3. Use the joy that God has giv - en, For the bat - tle keeping strong; Living

cheerful in the struggle, Praise the Lord, it won't be long.
most in pain or sorrow, Praise the Lord, it won't be long. } We shall sing,
near the gate of heaven, Praise the Lord, it won't be long.

### CHORUS.

We shall

We shall sing When the glorious fight of faith is

sing, We shall sing,

o - ver, Round the tree of life for - ev - er, Praise the Lord, it won't be long.

13

# 12

## Jesus, Bleeding One!

R. K. C.

"I am crucified with Christ."—Gal. ii. 20.

R. KELSO CARTER.

1. Je - sus, Bleeding One, save me From sin's in - ward breath;
2. Je - sus, Lov-ing One, hear me! Send de - liv - er-ance now;
3. Je - sus, Mighty One, touch me! Speak the word— Be clean;

Peace and lib - er - ty give me, Life instead of death, Let me cry in faith,—
Break the shackles that bind me, Bathe my heart and brow, At thy feet I bow.
In the fountain now plunge me, Lord, my spirit wean, On thy word I lean.

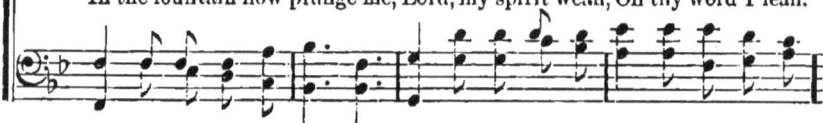

**CHORUS.**

Je - sus died for me, Jesus sets me free From transgression and inbred sin;

*rit.*

I with Christ have died, I am cru - ci - fied, Yet I live in him.

4 Jesus, Faithful One, help me!
Now, in grace, draw near:
With thy perfect love fill me,
Then, without a fear,
This my title clear,—

5 Jesus, Saviour, keep me!
Blameless from all wrong;
Sanctify me wholly,
Then, through ages long,
This my endless song,—

Copyright, 1886, by John J. Hood.

14

# Follow the Lamb.

Rev. Wm. Hunter, D. D.

Rev. J. H. Stockton.

1. O Je-sus, im-mac-u-late Lamb! Thy faultless ex-ample I see,
2. Thy word would I firmly be-lieve, Thy footsteps unswerving pur-sue,

And, conscious how feeble I am, For help look alone un-to thee.
Thy spir-it of meekness re-ceive, Thy will with all dil-i-gence do.

CHORUS.

Oh, follow the Lamb! Follow the ho-ly Lamb! To the
spotless Lamb, spotless Lamb,

liv-ing foun-tains he leads, Follow, oh, follow the Lamb!

3 Thy love in my heart shed abroad,
  A flame of pure loyalty there;
  A zeal for the glory of God,
  Kept burning by watching and prayer.
  Oh, follow the Lamb!

4 Thyself in my bosom enshrine,
  The Lord of my passions and will;
  And all my new nature incline
  Thy law with delight to fulfil.
  Oh, follow the Lamb!

5 No virtue of mine can I claim,
  No power to perform what I would;
  The virtue is all in thy name,    [blood.
  The power comes alone through thy
  Oh, follow the Lamb!

6 Oh, save me completely from sin,
  Oh, wash me, and I shall be pure;
  A thorough renewal within,
  A perfect and permanent cure.
  Oh, follow the Lamb!

# 14 Only Trusting in the Lord.

FANNY J. CROSBY.                                                      J. R. SWENEY.

1. Blessed thought that here be-low   Like a   riv - er peace may   flow,
2. Can I   ev - er   feel oppressed, When in   him is   per - fect   rest,
3. In my weakness   he   is strong, Can I   deem the   jour - ney   long
4. When his glo - ry   I   be-hold,   In a   world of   bliss un - told,

Peace that to   my   spir - it brings Visions bright of pur - er things, Visions
Can   my grate-ful heart re - pine, When his constant love is mine, When his
When he   leads me   by   his grace, While my faith his hand can trace, While my
There for - ev - er   to   a - bide,   I shall then be sat - is - fied, I shall

**CHORUS.**

bright of pur - er things.
con - stant love is mine.
faith his hand can trace.
then be sat - is - fied.

On - ly   trust   -   ing in the Lord,

On - ly trusting,                trusting in the Lord,

On - ly   lean   -   ing on his word,          This my joy to know that

On - ly leaning,          leaning on his word.

he Condescends my all to be, Condescends my   all to   be.

16

# 17 Healing for Thee.

FRANK GOULD.                                    JNO. R. SWENRY.

1. Je - sus the Sav - iour is pass - ing this way, Come, there is
2. Je - sus is pa - tient - ly call - ing to - day, Come, there is
3. Je - sus is pass - ing, oh, fall at his feet, Come, there is
4. Je - sus will save thee if thou wilt be - lieve, Come, there is

healing for thee; . . . . Rise at his bidding: oh, why wilt thou stay?
healing for thee; . . . . Now he is waiting, no long - er de - lay,—
healing for thee; . . . . Fly to thy refuge, thy on - ly re - treat,
healing for thee; . . . . Haste, and the rapture of pardon re - ceive,
yes, healing for thee;

*Fine.* CHORUS.

Come, there is healing for thee. . . . . Healing for thee, sinner, for thee,
yes, healing for thee.

D.S.

Now there is healing for thee; . . . Jesus the Saviour is passing this way,
yes, healing for thee;

19

DO RE MI FA SO LA SI

# De Shepa'd's Love.

Respectfully dedicated to Rev. CHARLES W. HARDENDORF.

JNO. R. SWENEY.

*Con espress.*

1. De mas - sa ob de sheepfol', Dat guard de sheepfol' bin, Look
2. "O," den say de hirelin' shepa'd, "Dey's some dey's black an' thin, An'
3. Den de mas - sa ob de sheepfol', Dat guard de sheepfol' bin, Goes
4. Den up t'ro' de gloom'rin' meadows, T'ro' de col' night rain an' win', An'

out in de gloomerin' meadows, Whar de long night rain be- gin— So he
some dey's po' ol' wed- da's, Dat can't come home a - gin, Dey's
down in de gloomerin' meadows, Whar de long night rain be - gin;—So he
up t'ro' de gloomerin' rain-paf, Whar de sleet fa' pie'c - in' thin, De

call to de hire - lin' shep- a'd, "Is my sheep, is dey all come in?" So he
los' an' good for nuf - fin, But de res' dey's all brung in," Dey's
le' down de ba's ob de sheepfol', Callin' sof', "Come in, come in," So he
po' los' sheep ob de sheepfol', Dey all comes gadderin' in, De

call to de hire - lin' shep- a'd, "Is my sheep, is dey all come in?"
los' an' good for nuf' - fin, But de res' dey's all brung in."
le' down de ba's ob de sheepfol', Callin' sof', "Come in, come in."
po' los' sheep ob de sheepfol', Dey all comes gadder- in' in.

# 19 Is it Well with Thee?

"Thou shalt keep therefore his commandments which I command thee this day, that it may go well with thee." Deut. iv. 40.

MARY D. JAMES.                    WM. J. KIRKPATRICK.

1. How prospers thy soul, fellow-pilgrim, Com-panion in life's dang'rous way?
2. Art thou a good soldier for Je-sus, Who gave for thy ransom his blood?
3. So strong are thy enemies round thee, So subtle the pow-er of sin,
4. Thine eye upon Christ, thy Commander, E'er watching, his orders to know ;
5. Do heaven's attractions grow stronger? Do earth's fleeting interests grow less?

Is  God thy de-fense and sal-vation? His law dost thou love to o-bey?
All  rea-dy to fight in the war-fare, Equipped with the armor of God?
So  weak is thy poor human nature, Yet, "mighty thro' God," thou may'st win!
And, faith-ful to fol-low his mandates, Dost on-ward vic-to-riously go?
Do  glories ce-lestial il-lumine Thy way through the dark wilderness?

CHORUS.

Is it well with thee? Is it well, is it well with thee? Is
with thee? is it well with thee?

God thy de-fense and sal-va-tion? Is it well is it well with thee?
is it well with thee?

## 20 All Things to me.

R. K. C.

R. KELSO CARTER

1. Je - sus my Sav-iour is all things to me, Him and him on-ly for-
2. Je - sus my Sav-iour is all things to me, From all my burdens he
3. Je - sus my Sav-iour is all things to me, Liv-ing or dy-ing, my
4. Je - sus my Sav-iour is all things to me, In fierc-est tri-als he

ev - er I see; Dai - ly with him I am walk-ing in light,
set - teth me free; Lean-ing on him I am ev - er at rest,
Lord, let me be Close to thy side, though the dread billows roll,
gives vic - to - ry; Conquers each foe and preserves me from harm,

CHORUS.

Cleansed from all sin and preserved by his might. I'm washed in the
Liv - ing in him I am mo-ment-ly blest.
Ev - er de - clar-ing, "'Tis well with my soul."
Shields and di-rects with his own might-y arm.

precious blood, Cleansed in the healing flood; Saved to the ut - ter-most,

walk - ing in lib - er - ty: Led by his staff and rod,

## All Things to me.—CONCLUDED.

*rit.*

Kept by the Son of God,—Je-sus my Sav-iour is all things to me.

---

**21** ## Loved and Redeemed.

S. MARTIN.

JNO. R. SWENEY.

1. O to be loved by him whose praise Angels on high are swell-ing,
2. O to be called his child and know I may be his for - ev - er,
3. O to be called an heir of grace Thro' his prevail - ing mer - it,
4. O 'twill be sweet to min - gle there, Finding each long-lost trea - sure,

*Fine.*

Loved and redeemed by him whose blood Purchased a heavenly dwell-ing.
Drawn by a sa - cred bond so strong Death cannot shake nor sev - er.
Heir to a home whose mansions bright I shall at last in - her - it.
Yet to be one in Christ my Lord Fills me with purest plea - sure.

D. S.—O, let my heart break forth in song, Casting its all be-fore him.

CHORUS.

*D. S.*

What can I do, oh, what can I do? How can my voice a-dore him?

23

## 22 I Trust in Thee Alone.

R. Kelso Carter.

Jno. R. Sweney.

1. Je - sus, my faith I now confess, Thy presence doth my spirit bless, Thou
2. No strength of mine I dare to claim, Be thine the glory and the fame, I
3. When dangers thicken round my way, And foes engage in bloody fray, Thou,

art my peace and righteousness; I trust in thee a-lone, O Lord.
rest on thine e - ter - nal name; I trust in thee a-lone, O Lord.
thou alone can win the day; I trust in thee a-lone, O Lord.

CHORUS.

O Lord, I stand upon the rock, Thy precious blood has washed my sins a-
O Lord, I stand up-on the rock,

way; With thee I walk in liv - ing light, That shineth
With thee I walk in liv - ing light,

more and more to perfect day.

4 'Mid friends that doubt and foes that
mock,
When lightnings fall and thunders shock,
Thou art my fortress and my rock;
I trust in thee alone, O Lord.

5 O, soon I'll stand on heaven's height,
Be crowned a victor in the fight,
Thyself my everlasting light;
I trust in thee alone, O Lord.

24

DO RE MI FA SO LA SI

# I'm more than Conqueror.

PARKER.                                                    R. KELSO CARTER.

1. I'm more than conq'ror thro' his blood, Je - sus saves me now;  I
2. Be - fore the bat - tle lines are spread, Je - sus saves me now;  Be-
3. I'll ask no more that I may see, Je - sus saves me now;  His
4. Why should I ask a sign from God? Je - sus saves me now;  Can

rest beneath the shield of God, Je - sus saves me now. I go a
fore the boasting foe is dead, Je - sus saves me now. I win the
prom - ise is enough for me, Je - sus saves me now. Though foes be
I not trust the precious blood? Je - sus saves me now. Strong in his

kingdom to ob - tain, I shall thro' him the vict'ry gain,— Je - sus
fight tho' not be - gun, I'll trust and shout, still marching on,—Je - sus
strong and walls be high, I'll shout, he gives the vic - to - ry,— Je - sus
word, I meet the foe, And, shouting, win without a blow,— Je - sus

saves me, Je - sus saves me now.

5 Should Satan come like 'whelming
    Jesus saves me now;      [waves,
Ere trials crush my Father saves,
    Jesus saves me now.
He hides me till the storm is past,
For me he tempers every blast,—
    Jesus saves me now.

# Will You Come.

CARRIE M. WILSON.                                                    JNO. R. SWENEY.

1. There's a message from the Lord,—will you come? Hear it sounding from his
2. He has tarried long for you; will you come? See his locks are wet with
3. Will you heed the Saviour's call? will you come To the feast prepared for

word,—will you come? Whosoev-er on his name will be-lieve  Life e-
dew: will you come? He a-lone your many sins can for-give; Will you
all, will you come? You will find him at the cross waiting there  With the

CHORUS.

ternal shall from him receive. He is calling you to-day—will you come?
look to him by faith and live.
garment that your soul must wear.                              will you come?

To the only living way—will you come?  Will you plunge beneath the flood
                             will you come?

of his all-a-toning blood? Will you be a child of God; will you come?

## 27 Blood of Jesus.

Rev. E. H. Stokes, D. D.                                    Jno R. Sweney.

1. Sal - va - tion! is the bat - tle - cry, Thro' the blood of Je - sus; Sal-
2. Sal - va - tion from all fears with - in Thro' the blood of Je - sus, From
3. .Sal - va - tion com-eth with a song, Thro' the blood of Je - sus; The
4. Sal - va - tion faith al - ways ob - tains Thro' the blood of Je - sus; Sal-

vation from sin's deepest dye, Thro' the blood of Je - sus; Lift the crimson
outward and from inward sin, Thro' the blood of Je - sus; Let the high cru-
victor's shout is loud and long, Thro' the blood of Je - sus; Ho! the cry of
vation from sin's last remains, Thro' the blood of Je - sus; Saved! the Spirit

banner high, All the hosts of sin de - fy, Vic - to - ry is always nigh,
sade be - gin, For our faith has always been, All the saints of God shall win,
saintly throng Like a riv - er flows a - long, Life to right and death to wrong,
now exclaims, Saved, a crown forever claims, Saved, a king forever reigns,

REFRAIN.

Thro' the blood of Je - sus. Thro' the blood, thro' the blood, Thro' the blood of

Je - sus; Vic - to - ry is always nigh, Thro' the blood of Je - sus.
Je - sus; All the saints of God shall win, Thro' the blood of Je - sus.
Je - sus; Life to right and death to wrong, Thro' the blood of Je - sus.
Je - sus; Saved, a king for - ev - er reigns, Thro' the blood of Je - sus.

Copyright, 1883, by Jno. R. Sweney.                    29

DO RE MI FA SO LA SI

# More and More.

R. K. C.

"The path of the just is as a shining light, that shineth more and more unto the perfect day."—Prov. iv. 18.

R. KELSO CARTER.
April, 1884.

1. The light of the Word shineth brighter and brighter, As wider and wider God
2. The wealth of the world groweth poorer and poorer, As farther and farther it
3. My waiting on Jesus is dearer and dearer, And stronger and stronger my

:S:

o- pens my eyes; My burdens and tri- als grow lighter and lighter, And
fades from my sight; The prize of my calling seems sur- er and sur- er, As
trust in his word: Without him I'm nothing, grows clearer and clearer, As

D. S.—tell the glad sto - ry from glo - ry to glo - ry, And

Fine. REFRAIN.

fair - er and fair - er the hea - ven - ly prize. Then shout halle - lu - jah to
straighter and straighter I walk in the light.
hard- er and harder I lean on the Lord.

shout hal - le - lu - jah to Him ev - er - more.

D. S.

Je - sus my Saviour! Oh, yes, hal - le - lu - jah to Him I a - dore; I'll

4 My joy in my Saviour is growing and growing,
As longer and longer I lie on his breast:
My peace, like a river, is flowing and flowing,
And fuller and fuller in Jesus I rest.

5 My praise and thanksgiving are swelling and swelling, [prove.
As broader and broader the promises
The wonderful story I'm telling and telling, [love.
And more and more sweetly I joy in his

## 29  Full of Glory.

G. R. STRICKLAND.

JNO. R. SWENEY.

1. O, my soul is full of glo-ry, and my faith is on the wing, Hal-le-
2. I am hap-py ev-'ry moment, for his presence gives me joy, Halle-
3. For the many precious seasons with my blessed Lord in prayer To his

lujah to my Saviour, halle-lu-jah! I am drinking full salvation from a
lujah to my Saviour, halle-lu-jah! But a nobler song of triumph will my
name be all the glory, halle-lu-jah! But to think that I shall see him in the

*Fine.*

nev-er-failing spring, Halle-lu-jah to my Saviour, hal-le-lu-jah!
heart and tongue employ, When I reach my Father's kingdom; hallelu-jah!
many mansions fair, Makes me shout aloud with rapture, halle-lu-jah!

D. S.—land of sweet repose, Going home to dwell with Jesus, hal-le-lu-jah!

CHORUS.

Go-ing home, . . I'm going home, Going home to dwell with
Go-ing home, I'm going home,

*D. S.*

Je-sus, hal-le-lu-jah! Where the crys-tal riv-er flows, in a

# 30 If you want a Loving Saviour.

W. L. T.

W. L. THOMPSON.

1. If you want a lov-ing Saviour, If you want a lov-ing Saviour,
2. If you want your sins for-giv-en, If you want your sins forgiv-en,
3. If you want to live a Christian, If you want to live a Christian,
4. If you want to go to heaven, If you want to go to heav-en

If you want a lov-ing Sav-iour, Ac-cept Je-sus now.
If you want your sins for-giv-en, Ac-cept Je-sus now.
If you want to live a Chris-tian, Ac-cept Je-sus now.
If you want to go to heav-en, Ac-cept Je-sus now.

**CHORUS.**

Oh, Je-sus wants to save you, In his arms he will receive you,

On-ly put your trust in his precious blood, He will save you just now.

By per. of W. L. Thompson & Co., East Liverpool, O.

32

# 31   We Overcome by the Blood.

R. K. C.             R. Kelso Carter.

1. Shout aloud, Hosanna to the King of kings! All my soul within me of his
2. In the smoke of battle, when the right seems wrong, Ever pressing onward with a
3. Resting by the waters, in a sweet ac- cord, Knowing all the joys that his
4. Marching, fighting, praising, in the storm and fire, Tried and tempted daily, we are

mer - cy sings; How the hymn of triumph to the heavens rings, When we
pur - pose strong, We will shout for joy,   for it wont be long Till we
ways af - ford; Vanished ev'ry pleasure, now we've seen the Lord, And have
lift - ed higher; Soon we'll join the chorus in the ransomed choir, Who have

### CHORUS.

o - vercome by the blood! Glo - ry! hon - or! Glo-ry to the Son of

God! Oh, praise him! praise him! For we o - ver-come by the blood.

   SPL-C    33

# 32 Never Give Up.

LIZZIE EDWARDS.                                                JNO. R. SWENEY.

1. Nev-er lay down the ar - mor; Oh, nev-er give up the strife;
2. Nev-er lay down the ar - mor; Oh, nev-er give up the cross;
3. Nev-er lay down the ar - mor, For dan-ger is ev - er nigh;
4. Nev-er lay down the ar - mor Till Je-sus shall bid us come

Meet with a daunt-less spir - it The tri - als and ills of life.
They who would fol-low Je - sus Must suf-fer reproach and loss.
Stand at the post of du - ty With watchful and sleep-less eye.
O - ver the si - lent riv - er To dwell in the conqueror's home.

CHORUS.

Though rugged and steep the path may be That leadeth the soul to God,

Remem-ber, the King of Glo - ry In sorrow that path has trod.

31

DO RE MI FA SO LA SI

# 33 A Child of the King of Kings.

R. E. HUDSON, by per.                                    ARRANGED.

*Not too fast.*

1. I know my sins are for - giv - en, My name is writ - ten down,
2. I know that Je - sus loves me, I'm sure I love him too,
3. I'm trust-ing ev - 'ry, mo - ment, His will is my de - light,

CHO.—I am a child of the King of Kings, His blood now cleanseth me,

He's promised me a man - sion, And I shall wear a crown;
And I am rea - dy wait - ing, His will and work to do;
My ev - 'ry need he doth supply, While walking in the light

I am a child of the King of Kings, I now have vic - to - ry;

I know he will be with me In ev - 'ry try - ing hour,
I know his pre - cious prom - ise He nev - er will for - sake;
In fel - low - ship with Je - sus, His blood now clean-seth me;

His love, his peace, his joy are mine; I'm walking in the light;

And I shall have the vic - to - ry Through his almigh - ty power.
He'll guide and guard me ev - er, And then at last he'll take.
Oh, glo - ry to his precious name! I'm free, I'm free, I'm free.

I soon shall see him as he is, Look on his face so bright.

35

## 34 The Clear, Flowing Fountain.

"If any man thirst let him come unto me and drink."

LIZZIE EDWARDS.                                                              JNO. R. SWENEY.

1. I have come from the clear, flowing fountain, Just come from the life-giving tide,
2. O, how oft I have gone to that fountain, O'er-burdened with labor and care,
3. O, the bliss of that clear, flowing fountain, That floats in a song on its breast.
4. By that clear, flowing fountain re-clin - ing, My soul from its casket would fly

And I heard the sweet voice of my Sa-viour, And saw him by faith at my side.
But how soon I for-got ev - ery tri - al, For Je - sus my Saviour was there.
Ev - ery murmuring wave-let re - ech - oes My Saviour's sweet promise of rest.
To the boundless and beauti - ful riv - er That rolls through the city on high.

### CHORUS.

If an - y man thirst let him come un - to me, And drink of the

wa - ter of life, said he; Oh, come to the fountain, Oh,

come to the fountain, Flowing, now flowing, flowing so free.

# 35 Buried with Christ.

Rev. T. Ryder, (chorus by R. K. C.)    Romans vi.    R. Kelso Carter.

1. Buried with Christ and raised with him, too, What is there left for
2. Ris-en with Christ, my glo-ri-ous Head, Ho-liness now the
3. Living with Christ, who di-eth no more, Follow-ing Christ, who
4. Living for Christ, my members I yield Servants of God, for-

me to do? Sim-ply to cease from struggling and strife,
pathway I tread; Beau-ti-ful thought, while walking therein,
go-eth be-fore, I am from bondage ut-ter-ly freed,
ev-er-more sealed, Not un-der law, I'm now under grace,

D.S.—Liv-ing in Christ and free from all strife,

*Fine.* CHORUS.

Simply to walk in newness of life. Buried with Christ and
He that is dead is freed from sin.
Reckon-ing self as dead in-deed.
Sin is dethroned and Christ takes its place.

Resting in him, my strength and my life.

D.S.

dead un-to sin, Je-sus him-self a-bid-eth with-in.

# Jesus, my Saviour and Lord.

R. K. C.                                                    R. KELSO CARTER.

1. I have found the dear-est friend, Je - sus, my Saviour and Lord;
2. Sins of crim-son turned to snow, Je - sus, my Saviour and Lord;
3. More and more up - on the way, Je - sus, my Saviour and Lord;

One whose love can nev-er end, Je - sus, my Saviour and Lord;
Thou hast paid the debt I owe, Je - sus, my Saviour and Lord;
Shin-eth to the per-fect day, Je - sus, my Saviour and Lord;

Now his gra-cious fet-ters bind All my be - ing, and I find
I have felt the heal-ing flood, Touched the wondrous cleansing blood
Brighter grows the heavenly dream, Now the gold - en glo-ries gleam,

**Chorus.**—Wondrous love and boundless grace! Such as I may find a place

D. S.

One with - in my heart enshrined, Je - sus, my Saviour and Lord.
Of the dy - ing Son of God, Je - sus, my Saviour and Lord.
In my heart He reigns supreme, Je - sus, my Saviour and Lord.

In the sun - shine of thy face, Je - sus, my Saviour and Lord.

# 37 Holy Spirit, Come.

ALEX. M. CARTER.                                JNO. R. SWENEY.

1. Precious Je - sus, Sav - iour dear, Set me free from slav - ish
2. May thy blood, for sin once spilt, Cleanse me from my crim - son
3. Bless-ed Lord, oh, bless-ed Lamb, Now I come just as I
4. May thy sanc - ti - fy - ing power Aid me in life's dark-est

fear, Fill me with thy per - fect love, Fit me
guilt, May its nev - er ceas-ing flow, Wash and
am, This my prayer, my on - ly plea, That thy
hour, Free me from the guilt of sin • Wash and

**Chorus.**

for a home a - bove. ⎫
keep me white as snow, ⎬ Ho - ly Spir - it, come, O
blood was shed for me. ⎪
keep me pure with - in. ⎭

Ho - ly Spir - it, come, O

come, Give me vic - to - ry, Wash me

Give O give me vic - to - ry,

in the cleansing blood, Sanc - ti - fy and perfect me.

Wash me in the cleansing blood, **39** Sanc - ti - fy and per - fect me.

# I Look to Thee.

R. Kelso Carter.                                                    Jno. R. Sweney.

1. My Lord, my Light, my Life, I look to thee; Through all the
2. When I would faint and die, I look to thee; Je-sus comes
3. Sun of my soul, my Light! I look to thee; Shining through

rag-ing strife Thy face I see. By foes and cares annoyed,
ver-y nigh To com-fort me; O - ver the waves of sin,
dark-est night Re-splendent - ly; Kin - dle the sa-cred flame;

The world seems but a void; Cast down but not destroyed, I look to thee.
Quelling the strife within; Lord, thou canst make me clean, I look to thee.
Now I the promise claim, Come thou in Jesus' name, I look to thee.

**CHORUS.**

Looking, yes, looking to Je-sus alone, Now may the blood be applied;

Looking, yes, looking to Je-sus a-lone, Je-sus, the Cruci - fied.

# At the Fount.

R. K. C.

R. KELSO CARTER.

1. At the Fount I stand, 'neath the bleeding hand, And beneath the
2. At the Fount the word of the dy - ing Lord, "It is fin - ished,"
3. At the Fount I find, when with willing mind To the Lord I

pierc - ed side; At the Fount with Christ, who was sacri - ficed, In the
loud proclaimed; And sal - va - tion's call sounds a - far to all,—Blind and
come to - day, That the flow - ing fount, in the ho - ly mount, Washes

**CHORUS.**

precious blood I'll hide. At the Fount, at the Fount, Where my
helpless, halt and maimed.
all my sin a - way. At the Fount, at the Fount,

Lord for me was cru - ci - fied; At the Fount, at the Fount,
At the Fount. at the Fount,

In the precious, speaking blood I hide.

4

At the fount I mean to be wholly
clean,
By the precious blood applied;
And my song shall be, to eternity,
Of my Jesus crucified.

# 40. Rest Found.

Rev. W. McDonald.

Jno. R. Sweney.

1. Rest for my soul I've found at last, A shel-ter from the win-try blast Of
2. In searching all the world around, No rest of soul like this is found, A
3. O rest divine! a rest of love Like to the rest the saints a bove En-

sin's de-structive power; With-in the Smit-ten Rock I hide, My
gift from heav-en above; A rest from guilt and in-bred sin, From
joy with Christ their king; 'Tis un-told bliss such peace to know, To

Saviour's o-pen, bleeding side, A strong, a might-y tower.
all the hat-ed foes with-in, From ev-'ry crea-ture love.
share the rest of heaven be-low, To love, a-dore and sing.

**CHORUS.**

Rest for my soul, Rest for my soul, I've found, I've found at last.

Rest for my soul, Rest for my soul, I've found, I've found at last.

# 41 The Angels are Looking on me.

Rev. John Parker.

J. P.

1. Like Ja-cob, in his Beth-el rest, The an-gels are looking on me;
2. Each night I lay me down to sleep, The an-gels are looking on me;
3. And when I wake, new toils to meet, The an-gels are looking on me;
4. A pil-grim to the heav'nly land, The an-gels are looking on me;
5. And 'till I reach my home at last, The an-gels are looking on me;

They watch my pil-low—I am blest, The an-gels are looking on me.
I know I'm safe, for an-gels keep, The an-gels are looking on me.
God's presence makes my joy complete, The an-gels are looking on me.
My steps are kept by God's command, The an-gels are looking on me.
With ev-'ry tear and tri-al past, The an-gels are looking on me.

**REFRAIN.**

All night, all night, The an-gels are looking on me;

All night, all night, The an-gels are looking on me!

43

DO RE MI FA SO LA SI

**42**

LIZZIE EDWARDS.

# Hiding in the Rock.

JNO. R. SWENEY.

1. I am hiding in the Rock, in the Rock of ag-es past, Trusting in the
2. I am clinging to the cross where my Saviour died for me, Trusting and be-
3. I am resting on the Rock, I am singing all day long, Singing of my

mercy that forevermore shall last; Oh, my soul has found a shelter from the
lieving that his face I yet shall see, For I know that to his promise he will
Saviour, for my heart is full of song; I have caught the holy rapture of the

*Fine.*

cold and chil - ly blast: I am hid-ing in the Rock of Ag - es.
true and faithful be; Oh, the blessed, blessed Rock of Ag - es!
bright and shining throng, Since I anchored on the Rock of Ag - es.

*D. S.*—I am hid-ing in the Rock of Ag - es.

CHORUS.

Hap-py in the Lord my Redeemer I re-pose, Happy in the peace that so

*D. S.*

ful - ly he bestows, Hap-py in the love like an ocean deep that flows,

44

DO RE MI FA SO LA SI

# 43 Unto him that hath loved us.

Rev. E. H. Smith.  H. Sanders. By per.

1. I have giv'n my all to Je-sus, And I live where the light doth shine; In the
2. I was once in darkness groping, I once roamed in the desert wild; But the
3. To the cooling fount he led me, To the pastures ev - er green; And my

world's deep gloom my hopes ever bloom, There is peace in this heart of mine.
Lord passed by, pouring light on my eye, And reclaimed me, his wand'ring child.
soul is restored, and shall boast in her Lord, For his blood hath washed me clean.

**Chorus.**

Un-to him that hath loved us, and washed ev'-ry stain, Un-to him the do-

minion and glo-ry be giv'n; O'er the world he shall come in his beauty to reign,

As he reigns in the brightness of heav'n.

4.
My faith, as the eagle, mounteth
On her pinion bold and strong;
And the world beneath is the sadness of
But above is immortal song. [death,

5.
O swift are the moments speeding,
And the land that is far away
Soon, soon shall be mine! and its morn-
Will dawn an eternal day. [ing divine

45

THEO. HYATT.

# I am the Light.

JNO. R. SWENEY.

1. { My path is dark, Lord, ver-y dark, No ray of light il-lumes my way;
A sweet voice whispers, Sad one, hark, . . . . . .

Oh, hear the blest Redeemer say:

**CHORUS.**

I am the light, I am the light, yes, I am the light,

I am the light, I am the light, yes, I am the light, Oh, walk in the light, oh, walk in the light, oh,

walk in the light, Then visions of bliss will break on thy sight, Break, break, break on thy
Break, will break, will

sight; And the path I shall lead will ev-er be bright, Ever, yes, ever be bright!

2  I'm burden'd, Lord, and sore oppress'd,
   I faint beneath the heavy load;
But Jesus says, In Me find rest;
   For all along the weary road,
   I am the light, etc.

3  I'm vile, Lord, very, very vile,
   And sin assails with mighty power;
A whisper comes, a heavenly smile,
   I'll cleanse thy heart this very hour.

4  I come, dear Lord, with ev'ry cloud,—
   My burdens all to thee I bring,
And cast my sins, with praises loud,
   On him whose wondrous grace I sing.

*Cho.*—Thou art the light! thou art the light!
   Forever, dear Jesus, I'll walk in this light:
Lo, visions of bliss now break on my sight,
   It is glory, all glory, my pathway is bright,
   Ever, yes, ever is bright!

# 45 Resting at the Cross.

W. J. K.

WM. J. KIRKPATRICK.

1. To the cross of Christ, my Sav-iour, I had brought my weary soul,
2. At the cross, while meekly bow-ing, Je-sus, smiling, bade me live;
3. At the cross, while prostrate ly-ing, Je-sus' blood flowed o'er my soul,
4. At the cross I'm calmly rest-ing, Ev-'ry moment now is sweet;

Burdened, faint, and broken-heart-ed, Praying, "Je-sus, make me whole."
"I have died for your transgressions, And I free-ly all for-give."
All my guilt and sin were cov-ered, And he whispered, "Child, be whole."
I am tast-ing of his glo-ry, I am rest-ing at his feet.

CHORUS.

Glo-ry, glo-ry be to Je-sus, I am counting all but dross,

I have found a full sal-va-tion, I am resting at the cross;

I'm resting (at the cross), I'm resting (at the cross), I'm resting at the cross.

47

DO KE MI FA SO LA SI

# 46 Night's Golden Stair.

J. E. RANKIN, D. D.

JNO. R. SWENEY.

1. Pillowed his head that night on a stone, Ja-cob lay down, all
2. Waked from night-vision, naught could efface Thrill of that hour with
3. Made he a shrine next morn of that stone, Nev - er a - gain to
4. Pa- triarch's God, my God be thou, too; Here, in Christ's name, my

friendless and lone; An- gels of glo - ry, in ans-wer to prayer, Came
God in the place; An- gels of glo - ry, could they be for - got, That
jour-ney alone: There worshipped God, with a vow and with prayer, Where
vows I re - new: Now by thy grace, Lord, my spir - it pre- pare, To

*D. S.*—An- gels of glo - ry, in ans-wer to prayer, Come

*Fine.* CHORUS.

down to his couch on night's golden stair. An-gels of glo - ry, with
God had been there, and he knew it not.
an- gels came down on night's golden stair.
build me a - gain the al - tar of prayer.

down to my couch on night's golden stair.

*D.S.*

wings sil - ver bright, Ascend-ing, descend-ing yon pathway of light,

DO RE MI FA SO LA SI

# 47 The Numberless Host.

F. A. B.

F. A. BLACKMER.

1. When we enter the portals of glo - ry, And the great host of ransom'd we see,
2. When we see all the saved of the ages, Who from cruel death partings are free,
3. When we stand by the beautiful river,'Neath the shade of the life-giving tree,
4. When we look on the form that redeem'd us, And his glory and majesty see,

As the numberless sand of the sea-shore, What a wonderful sight that will be!
Greeting there with a heavenly greeting, What a wonderful sight that will be!
Gazing out o'er the fair land of promise, What a wonderful sight that will be!
While as King of the saints he is reigning, What a wonderful sight that will be!

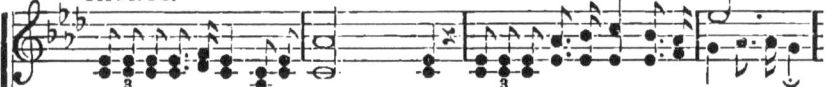

**CHORUS.**

Numberless as the sand of the sea - shore, Numberless as the sand of the shore;

Numberless as the sand,                    as the sand of the shore;

Oh, what a sight 'twill be, When the ransom'd host we see,

As numberless as the sand of the sea-shore.

SPL-D        49        DO  RE  MI  FA  SO  LA  SI

# 48 The Perfect Will.

R. K. C.                                              R. KELSO CARTER.

1. Thy will be done! to Jesus' feet With all my needs I glad-ly run; Lord,
2. Thy will be done! without, within, Lord, let me now all e-vil shun; For-
3. Thy will be done! break ev'ry chain; Speak thou the word, eternal Son; Cre-
4. Thy will be done! I bring my all, Without reserve, O Mighty One! On

make me now in thee complete, And let thy sov'reign will be done.
give and cleanse me from my sin, And let thy gracious will be done.
ate my spir-it, Lord, a-gain, And let thy mighty will be done.
thee, in sim-ple faith I call, Lord, let thy lov-ing will be done.

REFRAIN.

I pray thy will be done, Lord, I pray thy will be done, Thy

will be done, thy will be done, Thy will, O Lord, be done!

5 Thy will be done! I now believe;
  Soul, body, spirit, thou hast won;
  Disease and sin thou wilt relieve,—
  Lord, let thy perfect will be done.

6 Thy will be done! the flesh, the world,
  The devil, vanquished by the Son;
  In heart and life love's flag unfurled
  Proclaims, thy holy will be done.

## Jesus hath Died.

A. C. D.

Arranged by R. K. C.

1. Jesus hath died and hath risen again, Pardon and peace to bestow;
2. Sin's condemnation is o-ver and gone, Je-sus alone knoweth how;
3. Satan may tempt but he never shall reign, That Christ will never allow;
4. Resting in Jesus, a-bid-ing in him, Gladly my faith can a-vow,—

Fine.

Ful-ly I trust him; from sin's guilty stain, Je-sus saves me now.
Life and sal-va-tion my soul hath put on: Je-sus saves me now.
Doubts I have buried, and this is my strain, "Je-sus saves me now."
Nev-er a-gain need my pathway be dim: Je-sus saves me now.

D. S.—Je-sus saves me all the time; Je-sus saves me now.

CHORUS.

D. S.

Je-sus saves me now, Je-sus saves me now, Yes,

5 Jesus is stronger than Satan and sin,
Satan to Jesus must bow;
Therefore I triumph without and with-
Jesus saves me now. [in:

6 Sorrow and pain may beset me about,
Nothing can darken my brow;
Battling in faith, I can joyfully shout:
"Jesus saves me now."

---

50 MADAME GUION. Beloved Will of God.

Tune, "The Perfect Will,"
on opposite page.

1 Thou sweet, beloved will of God,
My anchor ground, my fortress hill,
My spirit's silent, fair abode,
In thee I hide me and am still.

2 O will, that willest good alone,
Lead thou the way, thou guidest best;
A little child, I follow on,
And, trusting, lean upon thy breast.

3 Thy beautiful, sweet will, my God,
Holds fast in his sublime embrace
My captive will, a gladsome bird,
Prisoned in such a realm of grace.

4 Within this place of certain good
Love evermore expands her wings;
Or, nestling in thy perfect choice,
Abides content with what it brings.

5 Upon God's will I lay me down,
As child upon its mother's breast;
No silken couch, nor softest bed,
Could ever give me such deep rest.

6 Thy wonderful, grand will, my God,
With triumph now I make it mine;
And faith shall cry a joyous Yes!
To every dear command of thine.

# 51 Alway.

R. K. C.          "Lo, I am with you alway."          R. Kelso Carter.

1. I'm walk-ing now in Beu-lah land, Where praises nev-er cease;
2. When-e'er the tempter's fier-y dart Is hurled with deadly aim,
3. Though storms in wildest fu-ry roll, They can not bring the night;
4. Up-on the clouds my Saviour rides, Up-on the waves he moves;

I feel the touch of Je-sus' hand, I know his per-fect peace.
I raise a-bout my help-less heart The shield of Je-sus' name.
For Je-sus shines within my soul In ev-er-last-ing light.
My soul beneath his sha-dow hides, My faith his prom-ise proves.

CHORUS.

Al-way, al-way,—The pre-cious as-sur-ance he gave:—

Al-way, al-way He's pres-ent and a-ble to save;

Al-way, al-way My rest in the prom-ise I make:

## Alway.—CONCLUDED.

My soul he will nev - er, No, nev - er, no, nev - er for - sake.

## 52 R. K. C. The Blood's Applied. R. Kelso Carter.

*Fine.*

1. { The blood's applied! my soul is free, I'm saved, without, with - in; }
   { The blood of Je - sus cleanseth me From ev - 'ry trace of sin. }

D. S.—blood's applied, I'm sanc - ti - fied, It makes me pure with-in.

*D. S.*

The blood's applied, I'm jus - ti - fied, It par - dons ev -'ry sin; The

2 I've bid farewell to every fear,
  By faith I claim the prize;
  Now I can read my title clear
  To mansions in the skies.

3 Temptations come and trials too,
  While hellish darts are hurled;
  But Jesus saves me through and
  In spite of all the world. [through,

4 Though cares and storms and sorrows
  About me thick and fast,      [fall
  My Jesus,—he is Lord of all,—
  Will bring me home at last.

5 Then will my happy, happy soul
  Tell of his love and rest.
  While shouts of victory shall roll
  From every conquering breast.

## 53 I. Watts. Am I a Soldier of the Cross? Tune above.

1 AM I a soldier of the cross,
  A follower of the Lamb,
  And shall I fear to own his cause,
  Or blush to speak his name?

2 Must I be carried to the skies
  On flowery beds of ease,
  While others fought to win the prize,
  And sailed through bloody seas?

3 Are there no foes for me to face?
  Must I not stem the flood?
  Is this vile world a friend to grace,
  To help me on to God?

4 Sure I must fight, if I would reign;
  Increase my courage, Lord;
  I'll bear the toil, endure the pain,
  Supported by thy word.

5 Thy saints in all this glorious war
  Shall conquer, though they die:
  They see the triumph from afar,
  By faith they bring it nigh.

6 When that illustrious day shall rise,
  And all thy armies shine
  In robes of victory through the skies,
  The glory shall be thine.

## 54. Back to the Fold.

Mrs. E. C. Ellsworth.

Jno. R. Sweney.

1. I heard thy voice calling me, Shepherd divine, I listened with gladness, and
2. I felt thy arms drawing me close to thy breast, I pillow'd my head there, and
3. Oh, keep me, watch over me, Saviour divine, Restrain and protect me, for

lo, I am thine! In doubt and in darkness no lon-ger I rove, But
sweet was my rest, As in from the mountain-paths dreary and lone Thou didst
now am I thine; And nev-er, oh nev-er, per-mit me to stray From thy

CHORUS.

sweet-ly and safe-ly I rest in thy love. O ref-uge most blessed, O
bear me re-joic-ing, and call me thine own.
cool qui-et pastures, thy safe fold a-way.

rest most serene, by waters the stillest, in pastures most green, O gentlest of

Shepherds, with thee would I stay, And wander no more from thy safe fold away.

DO RE MI FA SO LA SI

# 55 The Beautiful City of God.

MARY A. McKEE.                                          ADAM GEIBEL.

1. With mansions of fairness, And beau-ty, and rareness, And streets with a
2. Its riv-ers of gladness Will ban-ish all sadness, And sor-row shall
3. But light will be giv-en, All storm-clouds be riven, From o-ver that
4. No sor-row or sighing, Nor an-guish or dy-ing, Can sha-dow the

pavement of gold; Where no one grows weary,—No pros-pect is
van-ish a - way; The moon shall not lighten, The sun shall not
ci - ty of God; We'll view then in wonder, Thro' all that may
bliss of that home; And pilgrims who rest there, Forev - er are

**CHORUS.**

dreary,—And no one can ev - er grow old. Oh, there is a ci-ty, a
brighten, That ci - ty by night or by day.
sunder, The path that in sorrow we trod.
blest there, Nor yearn in their rapture to roam.

beau-ti-ful ci-ty, Whose builder and maker is God; A far - away

ci-ty, A wonder-ful ci-ty, The beau-ti-ful ci-ty of God.

by per.                               55           DO RE MI FA SO LA SI

## 53 He'll Take Thee as Thou Art.

FRANK GOULD.    JNO. R. SWENEY.

1. So great our Father's love, His on-ly Son he gave; And of-fered him a
2. In ten-der, loving tones His mercy pleads to-day, Then haste to bid him
3. He'll take thee as thou art, Then take him at his word, And give thyself this

ran - som, Our guilt-y world to save, And who-so-ev-er now Will
wel-come, No lon-ger turn a-way; Be-hold the cleansing stream, How
mo-ment To Christ thy gracious Lord; The who-so-ev-er will Is

on his name believe Shall nev-er, nev-er per-ish, But end-less life receive.
pure its waters flow, Thy sins, tho' red like crimson, He'll wash them white as snow.
sounding in thine ear, The shaft of death is flying, Thou canst not tell how near.

CHORUS.

His grace to all is free, O, wanderer, come and see The wonderful re-

demption pro-vid-ed now for thee, O, come and at his feet lay down thy

# He'll Take Thee as Thou Art.—CONCLUDED.

bro - ken heart, No matter what thy sin may be, he'll take thee as thou art.

## 57  We are Going Home.

WILL L. THOMPSON.

1. Je - sus my all to heav'n is gone, We are go - ing, go - ing home,
2. His track I see, and I'll pur - sue, We are go - ing, go - ing home,
3. The way the ho - ly prophets went, We are go - ing, go - ing home,
4. The King's highway of ho - li - ness, We are go - ing, go - ing home.

He whom I fix my hopes up - on, We are go - ing, go - ing home.
The nar - row way till him I view, We are go - ing, go - ing home.
The road that leads from banishment, We are go - ing, go - ing home.
I'll go, for all his paths are peace, We are go - ing, go - ing home.

CHORUS.

Sin - ner, you're in - vi - ted too, Won't you come and go a - long?

We are trav'ling to the bet - ter land, We are go - ing, go - ing home

By per of WILL L. THOMPSON, & Co.

# 58

# Look Above.

LIZZIE EDWARDS.

JNO. R. SWENEY.

1. Look above, oh, look above, Ye who toil and labor here,
2. Look away, oh, look a-way From the storm-y waves that roll,
3. Look beyond the winter's gloom, Look beyond its frowning skies;

1. Look above, oh, look above, Ye who toil and la-bor here,

See the morn - ing light of love Thro' the mist and clouds appear.
Where in realm of endless day Songs of rap - ture fill the soul.
Look beyond the silent tomb, To a spring that nev-er dies.

See the morning light of love Thro' the mist and clouds ap-pear.

CHORUS.

Look above where blossoms fair Wave a - mid the fragrant air;

Look above, where blossoms fair Wave amid the fra-grant air;

Look above, where all is love, Look above; your home is there.

Look above, where all is love, Look above; your home is there.

# 59. Abiding in Him.

Chas. B. J. Root.

Melody by D. C. Wright, arranged for this work.

1. A-bid-ing, oh, so wondrous sweet! I'm resting at the Saviour's feet;
2. He speaks, and by his word is given His peace, a rich foretaste of heaven!
3. I live; not I; thro' him alone By whom the mighty work is done:—
4. Now rest, my heart, the work is done, I'm saved thro' the Eter-nal Son!

I trust in him, I'm sat-is-fied, I'm rest-ing in the Cru-ci-fied!
Not as the world he peace doth give,'Tis thro' this hope my soul shall live.
Dead to myself, a-live to him, I count all loss his rest to gain.
Let all my powers my soul employ, To tell the world my peace and joy.

**CHORUS.**

A-bid - ing, a-bid - ing, Oh! so wondrous sweet!

A-bid-ing in him, I'm rest-ing in him, Oh! so wondrous sweet, wondrous sweet;

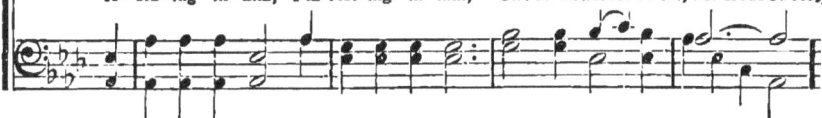

I'm rest - ing, rest - ing At the Saviour's feet.

I'm rest-ing in him, rest-ing in him, At the Sav-iour's feet, at his feet.

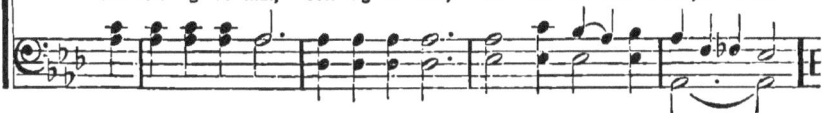

## 60 — Sanctified.

FRANCIS R. HAVERGAL.    "Sanctified in Christ Jesus."—1 Cor. i. 2.    R. KELSO CARTER.

1. Church of God, be-lov-ed, chosen, Church of Christ, for whom he died,
2. By his will he sanc-ti-fi-eth, By the Spirit's power with-in;
3. Ho-li-ness by faith in Je-sus, Not by ef-fort of thine own,—
4. He will sanc-ti-fy thee whol-ly; Bo-dy, spir-it, soul, shall be

Claim thy gifts and praise thy Giver!—"Ye are washed and sanctified!"
By the lov-ing hand that chast'neth, Fruits of righteousness to win;
Sin's do-minion crushed and broken, By the power of grace a-lone;
Blameless till thy Saviour's coming In his glorious ma-jes-ty!

Sanc-ti-fied by God the Fa-ther, And by Je-sus Christ his Son,
By his truth, and by his promise, By his Word, his Gift un-priced,
God's own ho-li-ness with-in thee, His own beau-ty on thy brow,—
He hath per-fect-ed for-ev-er Those whom he hath sancti-fied;

And by God the Ho-ly Spir-it. Ho-ly, ho-ly Three in One.
By his blood, and by our un-ion With the ris-en life of Christ.
This shall be thy pilgrim brightness, This thy blessed portion now.
Spotless, glo-ri-ous and ho-ly Is the church, his chosen Bride.

## Sanctified:—CONCLUDED.

REFRAIN.

Hal - le - lu - jah! what a Sav - iour! He who for our sin hath died:

Hal - le - lu - jah! what a Sav - iour! Now in him we're sancti - fied.

## 61  Reign, Lord Jesus.

R. K. C.                     Plantation Melody arranged by R. Kelso Carter.

1. Lord, I need thy sav - ing pow - er, And thy king - ly sway;
2. Thou art strong when I am weak-ness, Gird me for the fight;
3. Fill me now with joy in sor - row, Shine thro' ev - 'ry cloud;

Cho.—Lord, come quickly to thy king-dom; Reign, Lord Je-sus, reign;

*Fine.*

Thou my Ref-uge and my Tow - er, Hear me now, I pray.   O
Let me war with ho - ly meekness, Keep my ar - mor bright.
Touch with rainbow hues the morrow, Rend from death his shroud.

In my spir - it, bo - dy, soul, Reign, Lord Je-sus, reign.

4 Having now the life eternal,
   Conqueror in the strife;
   O'er the grave, in beauty vernal,
   Waves the tree of life.

5 We shall live with thee forever,
   Ransomed by thy blood;
   From thy presence parted never,
   Glory be to God!

# The Soul's Loss.

R. K. C.

R. KELSO CARTER.

1. A dreadful sound rings in my ears, The judgment thun-ders roll; A-
2. Be-fore me rise am-bi-tions vain, But should I reach the goal Of
3. If all the world, this ver-y hour, Were mine from pole to pole, There's
4. To him who gave I bring to-day A sac-ri-fi-cial whole; My

bout me swarms a host of fears For my im-mor-tal soul.
self-ish aims, what boots the gain If I should lose my soul?
noth-ing in its wealth and power To pay me for my soul,
all up-on the al-tar lay, Lord Je-sus, save my soul!

**CHORUS.**

For who-so-ev-er will save his life, the same shall certain-ly lose it; But

who-so-ev-er shall lose his life for my sake and the gospel's, shall save it;

For what shall it prof-it a man, for what shall it prof-it a man,

## The Soul's Loss.—CONCLUDED.

If he shall gain the whole world and lose his own soul, and lose his own

*rit. e dim.* **pp** *rit.*

soul? And lose his own soul? And lose his own soul?

## 63    The Lord Will Provide.

JOHN NEWTON.                                              Arr. by R. K. C.

1. { Though troubles as-sail    and dangers af-fright, }
   { Though friends should all fail and foes all u - nite, }  Yet one thing secures us what-

2. { The birds without barn    or storehouse are fed; }
   { From them let us  learn    to trust for our bread; }  His saints what is fitting shall

ev - er be - tide, The prom - ise as - sures us, "The Lord will pro - vide."
ne'er be de - nied, So long as 'tis writ-ten, "The Lord will pro - vide."

3.
When Satan appears to stop up our path,
And fills us with fears, we triumph by faith,
He cannot take from us, though oft he has tried,
The heart-cheering promise, "The Lord will
     provide."

4.
He tells us we're weak, our hope is in vain,
The good that we seek we ne'er shall obtain;
But when such suggestions our graces have tried,
This answers all questions, "The Lord will pro-
     vide."

5.
No strength of our own, nor goodness we claim,
Our trust is all thrown on Jesus' name,
In this our strong tower for safety we hide,
The Lord is our power, "The Lord will pro-
     6.                                        [vide."
When life sinks apace, and death is in view,
The word of his grace shall comfort us through,
Not fearing or doubting with Christ on our side,
We hope to die shouting, "The Lord will pro-
     *Chorus.*                                 [vide."
The foe we are routing, with Christ on our side;
We hope to die shouting, "The Lord will pro-
     vide."

# 64
## Only for Thee.

Eliza A. Walker.　　　　　　　　　　　　　　Jno. R. Sweney.

1. Precious Saviour, may I live On-ly for thee, On-ly for thee,
2. In my joys may I re-joice On-ly for thee, On-ly for thee,
3. Be my smiles and be my tears On-ly for thee, On-ly for thee,
4. Be my sing-ing and my sighing On-ly for thee, On-ly for thee,

Spend my pow'rs which thou dost give On - ly for thee, for thee;
In my choic-es make my choice On - ly for thee, for thee;
Be my young and rip - er years On - ly for thee, for thee;
Be my sick-ness and my dy-ing On - ly for thee, for thee;

Be my spir-it's deep de - sire On - ly for thee, On-ly for thee,
Meek-ly may I suf - fer grief On - ly for thee, On-ly for thee,
Be my peace and be my strife On - ly for thee, On-ly for thee,
Be my ris - ing, be my glo-ry, On - ly for thee, On-ly for thee,

May my in - tel-lect as-pire On - ly for thee, for thee.
Grate-ful - ly ac-cept re-lief On - ly for thee, for thee.
Be my love and be my life On - ly for thee, for thee.
Be my whole e - ter - ni - ty On - ly for thee, for thee.

64

DO RE MI FA SO LA SI

# 65 R. K. C.    Providence.    R. Kelso Carter.

1. The Lord is my rock, my fortress, my God, My strength, my defense, my
2. He wisdom is made and righteousness free, His love has secured re-
3. His statutes are right, re-joicing the heart; His mandates are pure, they

staff and my rod; My buckler, my tow-er, in him I a-bide; A
demption for me; He sanc-ti-fies wholly, the blood is ap-plied; A
light do im-part; His law is so perfect, his judgment so tried; His

**CHORUS.**

pres-ent sal-vation the Lord doth provide. The Lord doth provide, The
per-fect sal-vation the Lord doth provide.
promise so certain,—the Lord doth provide.

Lord doth pro-vide: He fail-eth me nev-er, The Lord doth provide!

4 When clouds gather fast, and light
  fades from view, [ings pursue,
When fears spring to life. and doubt-
From every temptation, or leading a-
  side, [vide.
A way of escaping the Lord doth pro-

5 My Lord and my God! my trust is in
  thee, [sea;
My peace floweth on like waves of the
O, dearer to me than all others beside
Is he who hath proven, the Lord doth
  provide.

6 I love thee, O Lord, my joy and my
  song, [long,
I rest in thy word, and, all the day
I sing of thy mercy, so wondrously
  wide, [provide.
Forever proclaiming, the Lord doth

7 By faith in his word I look o'er the
  tomb, [gloom;
The light breaks apace, dispelling the
Just over the river,—a home for his
  bride,— [provide.
A mansion in glory the Lord doth

   SPI.—E    65

# 66 R.K.C. Seeing God. R. KELSO CARTER.

*Andante.*

1. Lord, I see thee come, I hear thee calling now to me; I hear thy
2. Lord, I see thee die, I see thee dy-ing now for me; I hear the
3. Lord, I see thee dead, I see thee bu-ried now for me; I see my
4. Lord, I see thee rise, I see thee ris-en now for me; I hear the

precious speaking blood that floweth, Floweth now for me, I see the
cry, My God, my God, Why hast thou now forsak-en me? I hear thee
sins, my heart's corrup-tion, taken, Tak-en now from me: I feel the
Spir-it in-ter-ced-ing, In-ter-ced-ing now for me: I hear thy

way of life thy mer-cy showeth, Show-eth ev-en me.
shout the triumph song— 'Tis finished, Fin-ished, Lord, for me.
full-ness of the blood that cleanseth, Cleanseth ev-en me.
ten-der mer-cy sweet-ly pleading, Plead-ing now for me.

**CHORUS.**

I see thee, Lord, I hear thy word, I feel thy blood, thy cleansing blood : I

see thee, Lord, I hear thy word, I feel thy blood, thy cleansing blood.

# Oh! 'tis Wonderful.

E. A. BARNES.

JNO. R. SWENEY.

*Moderato.*

1. In the gospel's sweet old sto - ry, Lo! I read its gold - en theme,
2. Sin its se - cret work was ply - ing, Adding guilt with ev - 'ry day,
3. To his love I was a strang - er, To his call I gave no heed,

How the Prince of life and glo - ry came to suf - fer and re - deem.
Till I read that Christ in dy - ing, Died to take my guilt a - way.
Till at last I saw my dan - ger, Found the Friend I stood in need.

REFRAIN.

Oh! 'tis wonderful, won - der - ful, Yes, 'tis wonderful, won - der - ful!

Oh! 'tis wonder - ful, won - der - ful, The sto - ry of his love.

DO RE MI FA SO LA SI

# 68 What are we Doing To-day.

Laura Miller.

Jno. R. Sweney.

1. Oh, what have we done for the Master, And what are we doing to-day?
2. What, have we no buds for the Master? No fruit of our labor and care?
3. O Master, dear Master, forgive us, Unfaithful too long we have been;

Has any one, cheered by our counsel, Found comfort and peace by the way?
No sheaves that for him we have gathered, Who gives us each blessing we share?
But gladly we'll toil with the reapers, If thou wilt but help us a-gain.

**CHORUS.**

We speak of our hopes for the fu-ture, And tell of the fleetness of time;

But let us a-rise and be act-ive: The harvest is now at its prime.

DO RE MI FA SO LA SI

# Decide To-Night.

**"How long halt ye?"**—1 Kings. xviii. 21.

W. A. Spencer.

*Slow and with expression.*

1. Some go a-way from the house to-night, Pu-ri-fied from sin:
2. Some will go out from the house of pray'r, Harden'd by de-lay,
3. Some will go out from the house to-night, Full of trust in God,
4. Wait-ing a mo-ment more for thee, Je-sus still en-treats;

*Chorus.*—Go-ing a-way from Christ to-night, A-way from his loving care;

*Fine.*

Oth-ers re-ject the precious light, And go a-way un-clean:
Yielding to Sa-tan's lur-ing snare, Will hopeless turn a-way:
Hap-py in heart, made pure and white, By Je-sus' precious blood:
Soon will the knocking end-ed be, That now thy closed heart beats:

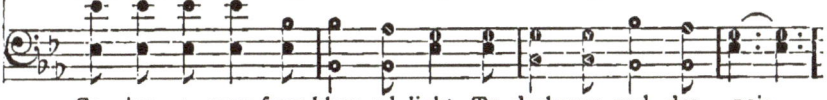

Go-ing a-way from bless-ed light, To darkness and des-pair.

Lov-ing-ly still the Sav-iour stands, Plead-ing with thy heart;
Nev-er-more shall the Spir-it plead At the bolt-ed door;
Go not a-way, poor wand'rer, stay Till thou too art free!
Stay, sin-ner, stay at Mer-cy's door, Seek the o-pen gate;

*D. C.*

Patient-ly knocks with his bleeding hands, Unwill-ing to de-part.
Now is the hour of thy soul's great need, 'Tis now or nev-er-more.
Walking with Christ life's hap-py way, Most bless-ed shalt thou be.
Sinner, de-cide, lest hope be o'er, And thou shouldst be too late.

DO RE MI FA SO LA SI

# 72 We Shall All Gather Home.

LAURA MILLER

JNO. R. SWENEY.

1. We are go-ing home to Je - sus: He is call-ing us a - way
2. We are go-ing home to Je - sus, And how happy we shall be
3. We are go-ing home to Je - sus, And we know 'twill not be long

To the mansions now pre-par - ing In the beauteous realms of day;
When the darkness shall be o - ver, And the morning light we see;
Ere we reach the land of promise, And behold the ransomed throng;

But the work that he has left us Must be finished ere we go; ere we go;
But the lonely we must comfort, And the fainting we must cheer; we must cheer;
But the dy-ing ones around us Need our watchful, loving care, loving care,

*Fine.*

We must reap a gold-en har - vest In the vineyard here be - low.
Let us work, and work in ear - nest, Till our bles-sed Lord ap-pear.
And our crosses and our tri - als Still with patience we must bear.

*D. S.*—To the mansions now pre-par - ing Soon we'll all gath - er home.

CHORUS.

*D. S.*

Then we'll all gather home, Yes, we'll all gather home;

DO RE MI FA SO LA SI

# Wait, and Murmur Not.

WM. J. KIRKPATRICK.

1. The home where changes never come, Nor pain nor sorrow, toil nor care; Yes!
2. Yet when bow'd down beneath the load By heav'n allow'd, thine earthly lot; Thou
3. If in thy path some thorns are found, O, think who bore them on his brow; If
4. Toil on, nor deem, tho' sore it be, One sigh unheard, one pray'r forgot; The

'tis    a bright and blessed  home; Who would not fain be  resting  there?
yearnst to reach that blest a - bode, Wait, meek - ly wait, and murmur not.
grief  thy sorrowing heart has found, It reached a   ho - li - er than thou.
day    of rest will dawn for thee; Wait, meek - ly wait, and murmur not.

CHORUS.

O,    wait,        meek - ly  wait, and mur - mur not,    O,
         meek - ly wait,

wait,        meekly wait, and murmur not,    O,    wait,
    meek - ly wait,                                      meekly  wait,

O,    wait,        O,    wait, and mur - mur not.
       meekly wait,                    O, murmur not.

By permission.

DO  RE  MI  FA  SO  LA  SI

# 74 Saved Through and Through.

Lizzie Edwards.

Jno. R. Sweney.

1. I was in bondage, but now I am free, I was in darkness, but now I can see,
2. Once I was thoughtless, but now I can say, Jesus has taught me to watch and to pray;
3. Filled with his fulness, my Saviour divine, All to his service I gladly resign,
4. Wonderful chorus, O joyful refrain, Saved by his mercy, the Lamb that was slain,

Per - fect the work of redemption in me, Yes, I am saved thro' and thro'.
Firm on the rock I am resting to-day, Saved by the blood thro' and thro'.
Filled with his fulness, what rapture is mine, Saved by the blood thro' and thro'.
Let me repeat it a-gain and a-gain, Saved by the blood thro' and thro'.

## CHORUS.

Saved by the blood of the Cru-cified One, Glo-ry to God! glo-ry to God!

*rit.*

Glo-ry to Je-sus for what he has done; Yes, I am saved thro' and thro'.

DO RE MI FA SO LA SI

74

# Ho, ev'ry one that thirsteth.

T. C. O'KANE.

1. Ho! ev-'ry one that thirst-eth,   Ho! ev-'ry one that thirst-eth,
2. "Come," saith the Ho-ly Spir-it,   "Come," saith the Holy Spir-it,
3. Come, ev-'ry one that hear-eth,   Come, ev-'ry one that hear-eth,
4. Come, whoso-ev-er list-eth,   Come, whoso-ev-er list-eth,

Ho! ev-'ry one that thirst-eth,   Come to the wa-ter of life.
"Come," saith the Ho-ly Spir-it,   Come to the wa-ter of life.
Come, ev-'ry one that hear-eth,   Come to the wa-ter of life.
Come, who-so-ev-er list-eth,   Come to the wa-ter of life.

**CHORUS.**

Come, for ev-'rything is read-y,— Je-sus is waiting; hear him call,

"Come and buy with-out mon-ey,"—"Je-sus paid it all."

DO RE MI FA SO LA SI

# 76 He that Overcometh.

R. K. C.  Rev. xii. 11.  R. Kelso Carter.

1. To him that o-ver-com-eth, To him that o-ver-com-eth
2. To him that o-ver-com-eth, To him that o-ver-com-eth
3. To him that o-ver-com-eth, To him that o-ver-com-eth

Will I give the tree of life, In the par - a - dise of God.
Will I give the hid - den manna, And the stone with the new, new name.
Will I give the power o'er the nations, And the Bright and Morning Star.

CHORUS.

O, we o-vercome by the blood, And the vict'ry of our faith o'er the world:
by the blood,

By the blood, and the word of our testi - mony; Oh! praise ye the Lord!

4 To him that overcometh,
To him that overcometh
White raiment shall be given,
And a name in the book of life.

5 Oh, he that overcometh,
Oh, he that overcometh
Shall be made a pillar in the temple,
And he shall no more go out.

6 To him that overcometh,
To him that overcometh
Will I grant to sit in my throne,
Even as I have overcome.

7 O, he that overcometh,
All things he shall inherit:
And I will be his God,
And he shall be my son.

# 77

# In Him Confiding.

Jno. R. Sweney.

1. The clouds hang heavy round my way, I cannot see,  I  cannot see; But
2. Thro' many-a thorny path he leads My  tired  feet, My  tired  feet Thro'

through the darkness I  be-lieve God leadeth me, God leadeth me; 'Tis
man-y-a path of tears I  go,  But  it is sweet, But  it  is sweet, To

sweet to keep my hand in  his While all is dim, While all is dim, To
know that he  is close to  me, My God, my guide, My God, my guide; He

close my wea-ry, ach-ing eyes, And  fol-low him, And  fol-low him.
lead-eth me and so  I  walk Quite sat-is-fied, Quite sat-is-fied.

77

DO  RE  MI  FA  SO  LA  SI

# Hallelujah to the Lamb.

SALLIE SMITH.　　　　　　　　　　　　　　　　JNO. R. SWENEY.

1. At the fountain, precious fountain, Jesus washed my sins a-way, Hal-le -
2. Hal-le - lu-jah, Jesus saves me, In my heart he reigns supreme, Hal-le -
3. I am trusting, ful-ly trusting In the power of grace divine, Hal-le -
4. Oh, the rest-ing, ho-ly resting! Not a shadow veils my brow, Hal-le -

lu-jah! hal-le - lu-jah! to the Lamb;　　And re - joic-ing in his
u-jah! hal-le - lu-jah! to the Lamb;　　And the brightness of his
lu-jah! hal-le - lu-jah! to the Lamb;　　Je - sus saves me now and
lu-jah! hal-le - lu-jah! to the Lamb;　　For the per-fect love of
　　　　　　　　　　　　　　　　to the Lamb;

*Fine.*

mer-cy, There I lin-ger all the day, Hal-le - lu-jah! to the bleeding Lamb.
glory Shines above the cleansing stream, Halle - lu-jah! to the bleeding Lamb.
ev-er, I am his and he is mine, Hal-le - lu-jah! to the bleeding Lamb.
Jesus, With its fulness fills me now, Hal-le - lu-jah! to the bleeding Lamb.

*D. S.*—Hal-le - lu-jah! to the bleeding Lamb,

**CHORUS.**

Hal-le - lu - jah! hal-le - lu - jah! My Redeemer, my Redeemer heard my

*D. S.*

call;　At the fountain, precious fountain, Praise the Lord, there's room for all;

heard my call.

　　　　**78**

# 79   I have entered Beulah Land.

FANNY J. CROSBY.     JNO. R. SWENEY.

1. Oh, my cup is ov-er-flow-ing With the goodness of the Lord;
2. From the sighing and the long-ing, That so oft my heart oppressed,
3. There's a pal-ace o'er the riv-er And its jas-per walls I see,
4. I have climbed the rugged mountain, But my Sav-iour led the way;

I am trust-ing in his mer-cy, And re-joic-ing in his word.
With my Saviour and Re-deem-er Now in per-fect peace I rest.
And among its ma-ny mansions There is one prepared for me.
Un-to him shall be the glo-ry, When I reach e-ter-nal day.

**CHORUS.**

I have climbed the rugged mountain,—On its summit now I stand; Hal-le-

lu - - - jah! hal-le-lu - jah! I have entered Beu-lah land.

Hal-le-lu-jah, hal-le-lu-jah,

79

DO RE MI FA SO LA SI

# Trusting only Thee.

LAURA MILLER.

JNO R. SWENEY.

1. In the rock of my sal - va - tion, In my ref - uge and my tower,
2. I am trusting and be - liev - ing Every promise thou hast made;
3. I am trusting in thy mer - cies, That are more than words can tell;
4. I am trusting, ev - er trust - ing, And my soul in faith is strong;

I am trusting ev - 'ry moment, I am trusting ev - 'ry hour.
I am trusting in the sunshine, I am trusting in the shade.
I am trusting in thy wis - dom, For thou do - est all things well.
I shall see thy face in glo - ry, And the time will not be long.

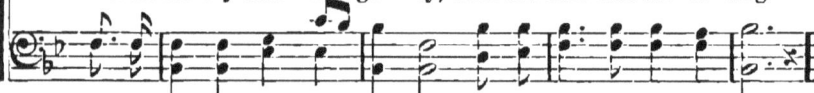

D. S.—O my Saviour and Re - deem - er, I am trusting on - ly thee.

CHORUS.

Trust - ing thee, on - ly thee, For I know thou lov - est me;

D. S.

## 81      My Unfailing Friend.     Key Eb.

1 Now I have found a Friend,
  Jesus is mine;
His love shall never end,
  Jesus is mine.
Though earthly joys decrease,
Though human friendships cease,
Now I have lasting peace;
  Jesus is mine.

Cho.—This Friend will never fail,
  Never fail, never fail.
This Friend will never fail,
  No, never fail.

2 Though I grow poor and old,
  Jesus is mine;
He will my faith uphold,
  Jesus is mine.
He shall my wants supply,
His precious blood is nigh,

Naught can my hope destroy,
  Jesus is mine.

3 When earth shall pass away,
  Jesus is mine;
In the great judgement day,
  Jesus is mine.
Oh! what a glorious thing,
Then to behold my King,
On tuneful harp to sing,
  Jesus is mine!

4 Farewell, mortality!
  Jesus is mine;
Welcome, eternity!
  Jesus is mine.
He my redemption is,
Wisdom and right-ousness,
Life, light, and holiness;
  Jesus is mine.

## 82 For me, for me.

1. {Jesus shed his precious blood, For me, for me;
   {Jesus brings me back to God, . . . . . . . Jesus saves me now.

2 There for me the Saviour stands,
  Shows his wounds and spreads his hands.

3 God is love, I know, I feel,
  Jesus lives and loves me still.

4 Plenteous grace with thee is found,
  Let the healing showers abound.

5 Rock of ages cleft for me,
  Now I hide myself in thee.

**84**  Is my Name written There?

**86**  Come to Jesus.

1 LORD, I care not for riches,
Neither silver nor gold ;
I would make sure of heaven,
I would enter the fold.
In the book of thy kingdom,
With its pages so fair,
Tell me, Jesus my Saviour,
Is my name written there?

*Cho.*—Is my name written there,
On the page white and fair?
In the book of thy kingdom,
Is my name written there?

1 COME to Jesus, come to Jesus,
Come to Jesus just now,
Just now come to Jesus,
Come to Jesus just now.

2 He will save you.
3 Oh, believe him.
4 He is able.
5 He is willing.
6 He'll receive you.
7 Flee to Jesus.

9 He will hear you.
10 He'll have mercy.
11 He'll forgive you.
12 He will cleanse you.
13 He'll renew you.
14 He will clothe you,

## 88 All the way long it is Jesus.

1. { O good old way, how sweet thou art! All the way long it is Je - sus; }
   { May none of us from thee de-part; All the way long it is Je - sus. }

CHORUS.

Je - sus, Je - sus, Why, all the way long it is Je - sus.

2 But may our actions always say
We're marching in the good old way.

3 This note above the rest shall swell,
That Jesus doeth all things well.

## 89 Victory. 7s.

*Fine.*

*D. C.*—Oh, how hap - py we shall be When we've gained the vic- to - ry!

CHORUS. *D. C.*

Vic - to - ry! vic - to - ry! We shall gain the vic - to - ry;

1 WHAT are these arrayed in white,
  Brighter than the noon-day sun?
Foremost of the sons of light;
  Nearest the eternal throne?

2 These are they that bore the cross;
  Nobly for their Master stood;
Sufferers in his righteous cause;
  Followers of the dying God.

3 Out of great distress they came;
  Washed their robes by faith below
In the blood of yonder Lamb,
  Blood that washes white as snow:

4 Therefore are they next the throne;
  Serve their Maker day and night;
God resides among his own;
  God doth in his saints delight.

5 He that on the throne doth reign,
  Them the Lamb shall always feed;
With the tree of life sustain;
  To the living fountains lead;

6 He shall all their sorrows chase
  All their wants at once remove;
Wipe the tears from every face;
  Fill up every soul with love.

## 90 — Come, Believer.

1 COME, believer, hung'ring, thirsting,
Come, a living sacrifice,
God will sanctify you wholly,
Cleanse and fit you for the skies.

Cho.—Come to the cross for full salvation,
Now the Comforter receive,
Perfect peace, and full salvation
God the Holy Ghost will give.

2 Now, believer, come and welcome,
God's free bounty glorify,
Come in faith and consecration,
All your fleshly hopes deny.

3 Lo! the Holy Ghost descending!
Now behold the cleansing blood,
Venture on him, venture freely,
Plunge beneath the crimson flood.

4 Christ the Comforter has promised
To the pardoned child of God,
Oh, believer, come and seek him,
Let your soul be his abode.

5 He will 'stablish, fix and keep you,
Rooted, grounded in his love,
Calm your wav'ring heart and seal it,
Seal it for his courts above.

6 Into all his truth he'll lead you,
All things teach you as you go,
In the dying hour be with you,
Death's dark river guide you through.

## 91 — Come, thou Fount. Tune above.

1 COME, thou Fount of every blessing,
Tune my heart to sing thy grace,
Streams of mercy, never ceasing,
Call for songs of loudest praise.

Cho.—Turn to the Lord, and seek salvation,
Sound the praise of his dear name;
Glory, honor, and salvation,
Christ, the Lord has come to reign.

2 Teach me some melodious sonnet,
Sung by flaming tongues above;
Praise the mount—I'm fixed upon it—
Mount of thy redeeming love!

3 Here I'll raise my Ebenezer;
Hither by thy help I'm come;
And I hope, by thy good pleasure,
Safely to arrive at home.

4 Jesus sought me when a stranger,
Wandering from the fold of God;
He, to rescue me from danger,
Interposed his precious blood.

## 92 — Oh, turn ye.

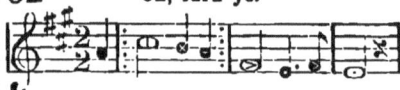

1 OH, turn ye, oh, turn ye, for why will ye die,
When God in great mercy is coming so nigh?
Since Jesus invites you, the Spirit says, come!
And angels are waiting to welcome you home.

2 How vain the delusion, that while you delay,
Your hearts may grow better by staying away;
Come wretched, come starving, come just as
you be,
While streams of salvation are flowing so free.

3 And now Christ is ready your souls to receive,
Oh, how can you question, if you will believe?
If sin is your burden, why will you not come?
'Tis you he bids welcome; he bids you come
home.

4 In riches, in pleasures, what can you obtain
To soothe your affliction, or banish your pain,
To bear up your spirit when summoned to die,
Or waft you to mansions of glory on high?

5 Why will you be starving and feeding on air?
There's mercy in Jesus, enough and to spare;
If still you are doubting make trial and see,
And prove that his mercy is boundless and free.

6 Come, give us your hand, and the Saviour
your heart,
And, trusting in heaven, we never shall part;
Oh, how can we leave you? why will you not
come?
We'll journey together, and soon be at home.

## 93 — Only Trust Him.

1 COME, every soul by sin oppressed,
There's mercy with the Lord,
And he will surely give you rest,
By trusting in his word.

Cho.—Only trust him, only trust him,
Only trust him now;
He will save you, he will save you,
He will save you now.

2 For Jesus shed his precious blood
Rich blessings to bestow;
Plunge now into the crimson flood
That washes white as snow.

3 Yes, Jesus is the Truth, the Way,
That leads you into rest;
Believe in him without delay,
And you are fully blest.

4 Come, then, and join this holy band,
And on to glory go,
To dwell in that celestial land
Where joys immortal flow.

## More Faith in Jesus.

Henrietta E. Blair.                                        Wm. J. Kirkpatrick.

1. While struggling thro' this vale of tears I want more faith in Je-sus; A-
2. To war against the foes with-in I want more faith in Je-sus; To
3. To brave the storms that here I meet I want more faith in Je-sus; To
4. I want a faith that works by love, A constant faith in Je-sus; A

*D. S.*—And

*Fine.* CHORUS.

mid tempta-tions, cares, and fears, I want more faith in Je - sus.
rise a-bove the powers of sin I want more faith in Je - sus.
rest con-fid-ing at his feet I want more faith in Je - sus.
faith that mountains can remove, A liv-ing faith in Je - sus.

this my cry, as time rolls by, I want more faith in Je - sus.

D. S.

want more faith, I want more faith, A clearer, brighter, stronger faith in Jesus;

Copyright, 1885, by John J. Hood.

---

## 95                    Beulah Land.

1 I've reached the land of corn and wine,
And all its riches freely mine;
Here shines undimmed one blissful day,
For all my night has passed away.

CHO.—O Beulah land, sweet Beulah land,
As on thy highest mount I stand,
I look away across the sea,
Where mansions are prepared for me,
And view the shining glory shore,
My heaven, my home, for evermore!

2 My Saviour comes and walks with me,
And sweet communion here have we,
He gently leads me by his hand,
For this is heaven's border-land.

3 A sweet perfume upon the breeze
Is borne from ever-vernal trees,
And flowers that never-fading grow
Where streams of life forever flow.

4 The zephyrs seem to float to me
Sweet sounds of heaven's melody,
As angels with the white-robed throng
Join in the sweet redemption song.

## 96 I hear the Saviour say.

1 I HEAR the Saviour say,
Thy strength indeed is small,
Child of weakness, watch and pray,
Find in me thine all in all.

*Cho.*—Jesus paid it all,
All to him I owe,
Sin had left a crimson stain ;
He washed it white as snow.

2 Lord, now indeed I find
Thy power, and thine alone,
Can change this heart of mine,
And make it all thine own.

3 For nothing good have I
Whereby thy grace to claim,—
I'll wash my garment white
In the blood of Calv'ry's Lamb.

4 Then down beneath the cross
I lay my sin sick soul,
I'm counting all but dross
Thy blood now makes me whole.

## 97 Are you washed ?

1 HAVE you been to Jesus for the cleansing
power?
Are you washed in the blood of the Lamb?
Are you fully trusting in his grace this hour?
Are you washed in the blood of the Lamb?

*Cho.*—Are you washed in the blood,
In the soul-cleansing blood of the Lamb ?
Are your garments spotless ? are they white
as snow ?
Are you washed in the blood of the Lamb?

2 Are you walking daily by the Saviour's side?
Are you washed in the blood of the Lamb ?
Do you rest each moment in the Crucified?
Are you washed in the blood of the Lamb?

3 When the Bridegroom cometh will your
robes be white,
Pure and white in the blood of the Lamb?
Will your soul be ready for the mansions
bright,
Are you washed in the blood of the Lamb?

4 Lay aside the garments that are stained
with sin,
And be washed in the blood of the Lamb !
There's a fountain flowing for the soul un-
clean,
O be washed in the blood of the Lamb!

## 98 I will sprinkle.

1 YE who know your sins forgiven,
And are happy in the Lord,
Have you read that gracious promise,
Which is left upon record !

*Cho.*—I will sprinkle you with water,
I will cleanse you from all sin,
Sanctify and make you holy,
I will dwell and reign within.

2 Though you have much peace and com-
Greater things you yet may find, [fort,
Freedom from unholy tempers,
Freedom from the carnal mind.

3 Be as holy, and as happy,
And as useful here below,
As it is your Father's pleasure ;
Jesus, only Jesus know.

4 Spread, oh, spread the joyful tidings,
Tell, oh, tell what God has done,
Till the nations are conformed
To the image of his Son.

5 O, may every soul be filled
With the Holy Ghost to-day ;
He is coming, he is coming;
O, prepare, prepare the way.

## 99 I am coming to the cross.

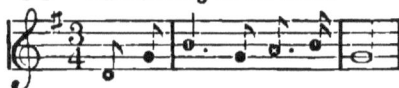

1 I AM coming to the cross,
I am poor and weak and blind ;
I am counting all but dross,
I shall full salvation find.

*Cho.*—I am trusting, Lord, in thee;
Bless'd Lamb of Calvary;
Humbly at the cross I bow;
Jesus saves me—saves me now.

2 Long my heart has sighed for thee,
Long has evil dwelt within ;
Jesus sweetly speaks to me ;
" I will cleanse you from all sin."

3 Here I give my all to thee,
Friends, and time, and earthly store,
Soul and body, thine to be—
Wholly thine for evermore.

4 In the promises I trust,
In the cleansing blood confide;
I am prostrate in the dust,
I with Christ am crucified.

5 Jesus comes, he fills my soul,
Perfected in him I am,
I am every whit made whole,
Glory, glory to the Lamb !—

# The Ark Floateth By.

Jno. R. Sweney.

1. Be-hold the ark of God, Be-hold the o-pen door, Oh, haste to
2. There safe shalt thou a-bide; There sweet shalt be thy rest; And ev-'ry
3. And when the waves of wrath A-gain the earth shall fill, Thine ark shall

REFRAIN.

gain that blest a-bode, And rove, my soul, no more. Oh, come, come to-
wish be sat-is-fied, With full sal-va-tion bless'd.
ride the sea of fire, And rest on Zi-on's hill.

day, do not long-er de-lay, The ark, precious bark, floateth by; The

waves as they roll Shall not cover thy soul, For Jesus thy Saviour is nigh.

By permission.

87

DO RE MI FA SO LA SI

# 101 The Glorious Hope.

CHARLES WESLEY.                                       R. KELSO CARTER.

*With animation.*

1. O glo-rious hope of per-fect love! It lifts me up to
2. Re-joic-ing now in ear-nest hope, I stand and from the
3. A land of corn, and wine, and oil, Fa-vored with God's pe-
4. O that I might at once go up; No more on this side

things a-bove; It bears on ea-gle's wings, It bears on ea-gle's wings.
mountain top See all the land be-low, See all the land be-low.
cu-liar smile, With ev-'ry blessing blest, With ev-'ry blessing blest.
Jor-dan stop, But now the land possess, But now the land pos-sess;

It gives my rav-ished soul a taste, And makes me for some
Riv-ers of milk and hon-ey rise, And all the fruits of
There dwells the Lord our Right-eous-ness, And keeps his own in
This mo-ment end my le-gal years, Sor-rows and sins, and

moments feast With Jesus' priests and kings, With Jesus' priests and kings.
Par-a-dise In end-less plen-ty grow, In end-less plen-ty grow.
per-fect peace, And ev-er-last-ing rest, And ev-er-last-ing rest.
doubts and fears, A howl-ing wil-derness! A howling wil-der-ness!

# 102 O for a Closer Walk.

C. WESLEY.

Tune, ORTONVILLE.

1. O for a closer walk with God, A calm and heavenly frame; A light to
2. Where is the blessedness I knew, When first I saw the Lord? Where is the

shine upon the road That leads me to the Lamb! That leads me to the Lamb!
soul-refreshing view Of Jesus and his word? Of Jesus and his word?

3 What peaceful hours I once enjoyed!
  How sweet their memory still!
But they have left an aching void
  The world can never fill.

4 Return, O holy Dove, return,
  Sweet messenger of rest!
I hate the sins that made thee mourn,
  And drove thee from my breast.

5 The dearest idol I have known,
  Whate'er that idol be,
Help me to tear it from thy throne,
  And worship only thee.

6 So shall my walk be close with God,
  Calm and serene my frame;
So purer light shall mark the road
  That leads me to the Lamb.

---

## 103  C. WESLEY.  The Blessed Hope.

Tune, "The Glorious Hope," on opposite page.

1 BUT can it be that I should prove
Forever faithful to thy love,
  From sin forever cease?
I thank thee for the blessed hope;
It lifts my drooping spirits up;
  It gives me back my peace.

2 In thee, O Lord, I put my trust,
Mighty, and merciful, and just;
  Thy sacred word is passed;
And I, who dare thy word believe,
Without committing sin shall live,
  Shall live to God at last.

3 I rest in thy almighty power.
The name of Jesus is my tower
  That hides my life above:
Thou canst, thou wilt, my helper be;
My confidence is all in thee,
  The faithful God of love.

4 Wherefore, in never-ceasing prayer,
My soul to thy continual care
  I faithfully commend;   [save,
Assured that thou through life wilt
And show thyself beyond the grave
  My everlasting Friend.

---

## 104  C. WESLEY.  For Purity of Heart.

Tune, "The Glorious Hope," on opposite page.

1 SAVIOUR, on me the grace bestow,
That, with thy children, I may know
  My sins on earth forgiven;
Give me to prove the kingdom mine,
And taste, in holiness divine,
  The happiness of heaven.

2 Me with that restless thirst inspire,
That sacred, infinite desire,
  And feast my hungry heart;

Less than thyself cannot suffice;
My soul for all thy fullness cries,
  For all thou hast and art.

3 Jesus, the crowning grace impart;
Bless me with purity of heart,
  That, now beholding thee,
I soon may view thy open face,
On all thy glorious beauties gaze,
  And God forever see.

83

## 105  Just as I am.

1 JUST as I am, without one plea,
But that thy blood was shed for me,
And that thou bidst me come to thee,
O Lamb of God, I come!

*Cho.*—We're kneeling at the mercy seat:‖
Where Jesus answers prayer.

2 Just as I am, and waiting not
To rid my soul of one dark blot,
To thee whose blood can cleanse each spot,
O Lamb of God, I come!

3 Just as I am, though tossed about
With many a conflict, many a doubt,
Fightings within, and fears without,
O Lamb of God, I come!

4 Just as I am—poor, wretched, blind;
Sight, riches, healing of the mind,
Yea, all I need, in thee to find,
O Lamb of God, I come!

5 Just as I am—thou wilt receive,
Wilt welcome, pardon, cleanse, relieve;
Because thy promise I believe,
O Lamb of God, I come.

6 Just as I am—thy love unknown
Hath broken every barrier down;
Now, to be thine, yea, thine alone,
O Lamb of God, I come!

## 106  The Child of a King.

1 MY Father is rich in houses and lands,
He holdeth the wealth of the world in his
    hands!
Of rubies and diamonds, of silver and gold
His coffers are full,—he has riches untold.

*Cho.*—I'm the child of a King,
The child of a King;
With Jesus my Saviour
I'm the child of a King.

2 My Father's own Son, the Saviour of men;
Once wandered o'er earth as the poorest of
But now he is reigning forever on high, [them,
And will give me a home in heaven by and by.

3 I once was an outcast stranger on earth,
A sinner by choice, an alien by birth! [down,—
But I've been adopted, my name's written
An heir to a mansion, a robe, and a crown.

4 A tent or a cottage, why should I care?
They're building a palace for me over there!
Though exiled from home, yet still I may sing:
All glory to God, I'm the child of a King.

## 107  The Great Physician.

1 THE great Physician now is here,
The sympathizing Jesus;
He speaks the drooping heart to cheer,
Oh, hear the voice of Jesus.

*Cho.*—Sweetest note in seraph song,
Sweetest name on mortal tongue,
Sweetest carol ever sung,
Jesus, blessed Jesus.

2 Your many sins are all forgiven,
Oh, hear the voice of Jesus;
Go on your way in peace to heaven,
And wear a crown with Jesus.

3 All glory to the dying Lamb!
I now believe in Jesus;
I love the blessed Saviour's name,
I love the name of Jesus.

4 The children too, both great and small,
Who love the name of Jesus,
May now accept the gracious call
To work and live for Jesus.

5 Come, brethren, help me sing his praise,
Oh, praise the name of Jesus;
Come, sisters, all your voices raise,
Oh, bless the name of Jesus.

6 His name dispels my guilt and fear,
No other name but Jesus;
Oh, how my soul delights to hear
The precious name of Jesus.

7 And when to that bright world above,
We rise to see our Jesus,
We'll sing around the throne of love
His name, the name of Jesus.

## 108  Blessed Assurance.

1 BLESSED assurance, Jesus is mine!
Oh, what a foretaste of glory divine!
Heir of salvation, purchased of God,
Born of his Spirit, washed in his blood.

*Cho.*—This is my story, this is my song,
Praising the Saviour all the day long. :‖

2 Perfect submission, perfect delight,
Visions of rapture burst forth on my sight,
Angels descending, bring from above,
Echoes of mercy, whispers of love.

3 Perfect submission, all is at rest,
I in my Saviour am happy and blest,
Watching and waiting, and looking above,
Filled with his goodness, lost in his love.

## 109. Jesus Bids You Come.

W. L. T.                                           W. L. Thompson.

*May be sung as a Solo.*

1. Jesus bids you come, Jesus bids you come, Now for you he's interced-ing,
2. Jesus bids you come, Jesus bids you come, Wea-ry trav'ler, do not tarry,
3. Jesus bids you come, Jesus bids you come, Voices may not always call you,
4. Jesus bids you come, Jesus bids you come, Where 'tis love and joy forever,

*pp*

Gent-ly at thy heart he's pleading, "Come unto me, Come un-to me."
Je-sus will thy burdens carry, Oh, will you come? Oh, will you come?
"Late, too late," may yet befall you, "Why will ye die?" "Why will ye die?
Where we'll meet to part, no, never, Sinner, come home, Oh, come, come home.

By per. of W. L. Thompson & Co.

## 110. The Sinner's Invitation.

*Fine.*

1. { Sin-ner, go, will you go To the high-lands of heav-en?
   { Where the storms nev-er blow, And the long summer's giv-en;
D. C.—And the leaves of the bowers In the breez-es are flit-ting.

*D. C.*

Where the bright blooming flowers Are their o-dors e-mit-ting;

2 Where the saints, robed in white,
  Cleansed in life's flowing fountain,
  Shining beauteous and bright,
  They inhabit the mountain;
  Where no sin nor dismay,
  Neither trouble nor sorrow,
  Will be felt for a day,
  Nor be feared for the morrow.

3 He's prepared thee a home,—
  Sinner, canst thou believe it?
  And invites thee to come,—
  Sinner, wilt thou receive it?
  Oh, come, sinner, come,
  For the tide is receding;
  And the Saviour will soon
  And forever cease pleading.

91

# 111  What Wondrous Love is This.

Altered and enlarged by R. K. C.

Arranged by R. Kelso Carter.

1. What wondrous love is this, O my soul, O my soul! What
2. When I was sink-ing down, O my soul, O my soul! When
3. He led me first to see What I was, O my soul! He
4. He keeps me day by day, O my soul, O my soul! He

wondrous love is this, O my soul! What wondrous love is this, That
I was sinking down, O my soul! When I was sinking down, Be-
led me first to see What I was; He led me first to see My
keeps me day by day, O my soul! I'm liv-ing at his side, Be-

caused the Lord of bliss To send this precious peace To my soul, to my soul,
neath God's righteous frown, Christ laid aside his crown For my soul, for my soul,
sin and mis-er-y, And then he set me free; Bless his name, O my soul!
neath the crimson tide, And Je-sus cru-ci-fied Keeps my soul, keeps my soul,

To send this precious peace To my soul.
Christ laid a-side his crown For my soul.
And then he set me free, O my soul!
And Je-sus cru-ci-fied Keeps my soul.

5 And when to Jordan's flood
   We have come, O my soul!
   And when to Jordan's flood
   We have come;
Jehovah rules the tide,
The water he'll divide,
And welcome home his Bride,
   Praise the Lord, O my soul!
And welcome home his Bride,
   O my soul!

*[Additional verses on opposite page.]*

# 112 Jesus, Blessed Saviour.

CHARLES H. ELLIOTT.     A. M. WORTMAN, M. D.

1. All my sins were laid on thee, Je - sus, bles - sed Sav - iour;
2. I have noth - ing else to bring, Je - sus, bles - sed Sav - iour;
3. Thro' my faith in thy dear name, Je - sus, bles - sed Sav - iour,
4. 'Tis thy mer - cy I implore, Je - sus, bles - sed Sav - iour;

*Fine.*

Thou didst bear them all for me, Je - sus, bles - sed Sav - iour.
Poor and weak, to thee I cling, Je - sus, bles - sed Sav - iour.
Let me now thy prom - ise claim, Je - sus, bles - sed Sav - iour.
Close not yet the o - pen door, Je - sus, bles - sed Sav - iour.

*D. S.*—Cleanse, forgive, and seal it thine, Je - sus, bles - sed Sav - iour.

CHORUS.     *D. S.*

Take this bro - ken heart of mine, By thy blood, thy grace di - vine,

*[Concluded from opposite page.]*

6 There we shall meet again
  Those we love, O my soul!
There we shall meet again
  Those we love;
The meeting will be sweet,
At the dear Redeemer's feet;
Our joy shall be complete,
  O my soul, O my soul!
Our joy shall be complete,
  O my soul!

7 Then with the ransomed throng,
  O my soul, O my soul!
Then with the ransomed throng,
  O my soul!
Then with the ransomed throng,
Redeemed through ages long,
We'll sing the new, new song,
  Praise the Lord, O my soul!
We'll sing the new, new song,
  O my soul!

# 113 At the Cross.

R. Kelso Carter.

Arr. by E. E. Nickerson.

1. O Je-sus, Lord, thy dy-ing love Hath pierced my con-trite heart;
2. A-mid the night of sin and death Thy light hath filled my soul;
3. I kiss thy feet, I clasp thy hand, I touch thy bleed-ing side;
4. My Lord, my light, my strength, my all, I count my gain but loss;

Now take my life, and let me prove How dear to me thou art.
To me thy lov-ing voice now saith, Thy faith hath made thee whole.
O let me here for-ev-er stand, Where thou wast cru-ci-fied.
For-ev-er let thy love enthrall, And keep me at the cross.

**CHORUS.**

At the cross, at the cross, where I first saw the light, And the burden of my heart roll'd a-way, It was there by faith I receiv'd my sight, And now I am hap-py night and day!

# 114    Resting.

FRANCES R. HAVERGAL.

J. R. SWENEY.

*Not too fast.*

1. Rest-ing on the faithfulness of Christ our Lord, Rest-ing on the
2. Rest-ing 'neath his guiding hand for un-track'd days, Rest-ing 'neath his
3. Rest-ing in the fort-ress while the foe is nigh, Rest-ing in the
4. Rest-ing in the pastures and beneath the Rock, Rest-ing by the

ful-ness of his own sure word. Resting on his pow-er, on his love untold,
shad-ow from the noontide rays; Resting at the e-ventide beneath his wing,
life-boat while the waves roll high, Resting in his char-iot for the swift glad race,
wa-ters where he leads his flock, Resting, while we lis-ten at his glorious feet,

D. S.—Rest-ing and re-joic-ing, let his saved ones sing,

**CHORUS.**

Rest-ing on his cov-e-nant se-cured of old.
In the fair pa-vil-ion of our Saviour King.
Rest-ing, al-ways resting in his boundless grace.
Rest-ing in his ver-y arms! O, rest com-plete.

Rest-ing and be-

Glo-ry, glo-ry, glo-ry be to Christ our King.

*D.S.*

liev-ing, let us onward press, Resting in himself, the Lord our righteousness;

# 115    Oh, Jesus, Jesus.

Rev. F. W. Faber, (Chorus by R. K. C.)      Arr. from Taubert by R. Kelso Carter.

1. Oh, Je - sus, Je - sus, dear - est Lord! Forgive me if I say,
2. I love thee so I know not how My transports to con - trol;
3. For thou to me art all in all; My hon - or and my wealth;

For ver - y love, thy sa - cred name A thou - sand times a day.
Thy love is like a burn - ing fire With - in my ver - y soul.
My heart's de - sire, my bo - dy's strength, My soul's e - ter - nal health.

**CHORUS.**

Oh, Je - sus, Lord, with me a - bide; I rest in thee, whate'er be - tide;

*rit.*

Thy gra - cious smile is my re - ward; I love, I love thee, Lord!

4 Burn, burn, O love, within my heart,
Burn fiercely night and day,
Till all the dross of earthly loves
Is burned, and burned away.

5 O light in darkness, joy in grief,
O heaven begun on earth;
Jesus, my love, my treasure, who
Can tell what thou art worth?

Copyright, 1886, by John J. Hood.

96

# 116

## Life Everlasting.

R. Kelso Carter.

A. M. Wortman, M. D.

*Animated.*

1. Trusting in Jesus there's release from sin, Par-don and puri-ty, and
2. Peace in believ-ing is the sure re-ward, When trusting simply in our
3. Cleansed by the precious blood I now have rest, Sit-ting at Jesus' feet I'm
4. Walking in spir-it, from the flesh set free, No condemna-tion is there

peace with - in; He who will trust a-lone in Christ to win,
gra - cious Lord; He that be-liev-eth in the might-y Word,
dai - ly blest, Strong in the Word, by sov'reign love expressed,—
now for me; Shin-ing thro' ev-'ry cloud the words I see,—

CHORUS.

Hath ev - er-last-ing life. O, believe, O be-lieve, and re-

ceive, and re-ceive, Perfect peace in place of strife; O be-lieve, for

He that believ-eth on the Son of God Hath ev-erlast-ing life.

SPL-G    97

# 117 I am His and He is Mine.

**"I am my beloved's and my beloved is mine."—CANT. vi : 3.** JNO. R. SWENEY.

1. Loved with everlasting love, Led by grace that love to know, Spirit, breathing
2. Heaven above is softer blue, Earth around is sweeter green; Something lives in
3. Things that once caused wild alarm Cannot now disturb my rest; Closed in ever-
4. His for-ev-er, on-ly his! Who the Lord and me can part? Ah, with what a

from above, Thou hast taught me it is so.    Oh, this full and per-fect peace!
ev-ery hue, Christless eyes have never seen; Birds with gladder songs o'er flow,
last-ing arms, Pillowed on his loving breast.    Oh, to lie for-ev-er here,
rest of bliss Christ can fill the loving heart! Heaven and earth may fade and flee,

Oh, this transport all divine!    In    a love which can-not cease, I    am
Flowers with deeper beauty shine;    Since I know, as now I know, I    am
Care and doubt and self resign;    While he whispers in my ear I    am
First-born light in gloom decline;    But while God and I shall be, I    am

**CHORUS**

his and he  is   mine.
his and he  is   mine.
his and he  is   mine.    I  am my be-lov-ed's and my be-lov-ed is
his and he  is   mine.

mine,    I 'am my be-lov-ed's and my be-lov-ed is    mine.

# Where the Living Waters Flow.

EDWARD E. NICKERSON, by per.

1. Rest to the wea-ry soul And ach-ing breast is given,
2. For thee, my soul, for thee These price-less joys were bought,
3. Come, with the ransomed train, The Sa-viour's prais-es sing,
4. And soon, be-fore his face, We'll praise in light a-bove,

Down where the liv-ing wa-ters flow; Grace makes the wounded whole,
Down where the liv-ing wa-ters flow; Thine is the mer-cy free,
Down where the liv-ing wa-ters flow; Re-joice! the Lamb was slain,
Down where the liv-ing wa-ters flow; Tri-umphant through his grace,

Love fills our heart with heaven, Down where the liv-ing waters flow.
That Christ to earth has brought, Down where the liv-ing waters flow.
A-dore! he reigns a King, Down where the liv-ing waters flow.
Made per-fect by his love, Down where the liv-ing waters flow.

**CHORUS.**

Down where the living waters flow, Down where the tree of life doth grow, I'm

liv-ing in the light, for Je-sus now I fight, Down where the living waters flow.

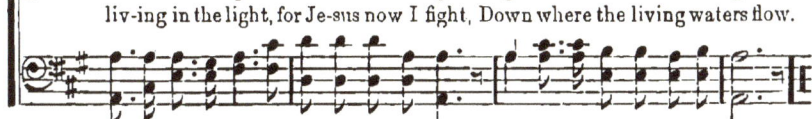

# 119 O, Sing of the Rapture.

FRANK GOULD.

JNO. R. SWENEY.

1. O sing of the rap-ture, the ho-ly de-light, Sal-va-tion so
2. O sing of the ful-ness of in-fi-nite love, The bliss that we
3. How sweet when we gath-er to wor-ship his name, And praise him for
4. O glo-ry to Je-sus! a-gain and a-gain Our song of de-

free-ly be-stows, Our path, like the noonday, is cloudless and bright With
constantly share, Com-mun-ing with Jesus our Sa-viour a-bove, And
all he has done, To feel, while the riches of grace we proclaim, Our
vo-tion shall rise, And an-gels re-ech-o the joy-ful a-men They

CHORUS.

joy from his presence that flows. }
knowing our treasure is there. }
E-den on earth is be-gun. } Sal-va-tion is free, sal-va-tion is free,
bear from our hearts to the skies. }

A per-fect sal-va-tion for you and for me; When o-ver the riv-er our

dwell-ing we see, We'll shout as we en-ter, sal-va-tion is free.

# 120. Standing on the Promises.

R. K. C.

R. Kelso Carter.

1. Standing on the prom-is - es of Christ my King, Thro' e - ter - nal
2. Standing on the prom-is - es that can - not fail, When the howling
3. Standing on the prom-is - es I now can see Per-fect, present
4. Standing on the prom-is - es of Christ the Lord, Bound to him e -
5. Standing on the prom-is - es I can - not fall, Listening ev - ery

a - ges let his prais-es ring; Glo - ry in the highest, I will shout and sing,
storms of doubt and fear as-sail, By the liv - ing Word of God I shall pre - vail,
cleansing in the blood for me; Standing in the liberty where Christ makes free,
ter - nally by love's strong cord, O - vercoming dai - ly with the Spir-its' sword,
moment to the Spir-its' call, Rest-ing in my Saviour, as my all in all,

**CHORUS.**

Stand - ing, Stand - ing,
Standing on the promises of God. Standing on the promise, Standing on the promise,

Stand - - ing,
Standing on the prom-is - es of God my Saviour; Standing on the promise,

Stand - - ing,
Standing on the promise, I'm standing on the prom-is - es of God.

Copyright, 1886, by John J. Hood.

101

# The Glad Redemption Song.

R. Kelso Carter.                                                      A. M. Wortman, M. D.

1. I'm saved by the blood, O, praise the Lord! And Je - sus' smile is
2. I'm saved! how my soul with rapture thrills! The peace of God my
3. I'm saved! O my soul, with cour- age fight 'Gainst fear- ful odds, in
4. I'm saved by the blood from death and sin; I'm washed without and

my re - ward; With the church of God—a might - y throng—I will
be - ing fills; The light of heaven shines clear and strong As I
dark - est night; Strong in faith, look up, it wont be long; Shout a-
cleansed with - in; And the Lord can keep my soul from wrong While I

**CHORUS.**

sing the glad redemption song.
sing the sweet redemption song. For I'm saved by the blood, Yes, I'm
loud the great redemption song.
sing the grand redemption song.         yes, I'm saved,        by the blood,

saved by the blood of the Lamb, And I'll sing, yes, I'll sing I'll sing The
of the Lamb,

glad redemption song, I am saved by the blood of the Lamb. of the Lamb.

# 122    Wrestling Jacob.

CHARLES WESLEY.            WM. J. KIRKPATRICK.

1. Come, O thou Trav-el-ler unknown, Whom still I hold, but cannot see;
2. I need not tell thee who I am; My sin and mis-er-y declare;
3. In vain thou strugglest to get free; I nev-er will unloose my hold:

My com-pa-ny be-fore is gone, And I am left alone with thee:
Thyself hast called me by my name; Look on thy hands, and read it there;
Art thou the Man that died for me? The se-cret of thy love un-fold:

With thee all night I mean to stay, And wrestle till the break of day,
But who, I ask thee, who art thou? Tell me thy name, and tell me now,
Wrestling, I will not let thee go, Till I thy name, thy nature know,

With thee all night I mean to stay, And wrestle till the break of day.
But who, I ask thee, who art thou? Tell me thy name, and tell me now.
Wrestling, I will not let thee go, Till I thy name, thy nature know.

5 Wilt thou not yet to me reveal
    Thy new, unutterable name?
Tell me, I still beseech thee, tell;
    To know it now resolved I am:
Wrestling, I will not let thee go,
Till I thy name, thy nature know.

6 What tho' my shrinking flesh complain,
    And murmur to contend so long?
I rise superior to my pain:
    When I am weak, then I am strong!
And when my all of strength shall fail,
I shall with the God-man prevail.

# 123 My All in All.

R. K. C.                                    Plantation Melody, alt. and arr. by R. K. Carter.

1. I'm trust - ing, I'm trust - ing, I'm trust - ing in Je - sus to
2. I'm rest - ing, I'm rest - ing, I'm rest - ing my bur - dens on
3. I'm walk - ing, I'm walk - ing, I'm walk - ing with Je - sus each
4. I'm hold - ing, I'm hold - ing, I'm hold - ing the hand of my

D. C.—For I'm go - ing, I'm go - ing, I'm go - ing to glo - ry with

save me; I'm trust - ing, I'm trust - ing In him, my all in all.
Je - sus; I'm rest - ing, I'm rest - ing On him, my all in all.
mo - ment; I'm walk - ing, I'm walk - ing With him, my all in all.
Sa - viour; I'm hold - ing, I'm hold - ing To him, my all in all.

Je - sus; I'm go - ing, I'm go - ing with him my all in all.

*Fine.*

**CHORUS.**

Come, brothers, won't you join me? Come, brothers, won't you join me to - day?

Come, brothers, won't you join me? Won't you join me in the army of the Lord?

*D.C.*

# 124 Coming Judgment.

"Flee from the wrath of God."

R. K. C.

Plantation Melody, alt. and arr. by R. KELSO CARTER.

1. O, the rocks and the mountains shall all flee a-way, When Je-sus comes to
2. In the world there's no pleasure can ever endure, The moments are so
3. In the blood there is cleansing without and within, And Je-sus breaks the

judgment the last great day; And no ref-uge can shel-ter, no
fleet-ing, there's noth-ing sure; For we fade as a leaf and our
pow-er of can-celled sin; He keeps us and saves us to

cov-ert can hide The soul that hath re-ject-ed the cru-ci-fied.
time's but a breath, The Lord hath said the wa-ges of sin is death.
the ut-termost, Bap-tiz-es us with fire and the Ho-ly Ghost.

**CHORUS.**

Sin-ner, sin-ner, plunge in the crim-son flood! There's

pardon, peace, and cleansing be-neath the blood, neath the blood.

## 125 He healeth me.

1 HE healeth me, O bless his name!
I want to spread abroad his fame;
From dread disease he sets me free,
The Lord my healer, strong is he.

Cho.—He healeth me, he healeth me,
By power divine he healeth me;
He healed the sick in Galilee,
And now by faith he healeth me.

2 He healeth me, my simple faith
Believes the word that Jesus saith,
And takes the place of ardent hope,
Believes the Lord will raise me up.

3 He healeth me, I touch for cure
The border of his garment pnre,
And virtue through my being flows,
A healing balm for nature's woes.

4 He healeth me, as when of yore,
Their sins and sicknesses he bore,
Nor has he lost his power and skill,
Our blessed Christ is living still.

5 He healeth me, O oft I sought
This healing power, but found it not,
But now I trust, with all my soul,
And now thro' faith he makes me whole.

## 126 How Sweet the Name.

1 HOW sweet the name of Jesus sounds
In a believer's ear;
It soothes his so-rows, heals his wounds,
And drives away his fear.

Cho.—I do believe, I now believe
That Jesus died for me,
And through his blood his precious
I am from sin set free. [blood,

2 It makes the wounded spirit whole,
And calms the troubled breast;
'Tis manna to the hungry soul,
And to the weary, rest.

3 Dear Name, the Rock on which I build,
My shield and hiding-place;
My never-failing treasure, filled
With boundless stores of grace.

4 Jesus my Shepherd, Saviour, Friend,
My Prophet, Priest, and King,
My Lord, my Life, my Way, my End,
Accept the praise I bring.

5 I would thy boundless love proclaim
With every fleeting breath;
So shall the music of thy name
Refresh my soul in death.

## 127 I know I love Thee better.

1 I KNOW I love thee better, Lord,
Than any earthly joy,
For thou hast given me the peace
Which nothing can destroy.

Cho.—The half has never yet been told,
Of love so full and free;
The half has never yet been told,
The blood—it cleanseth me.

2 I know that thou art nearer still
Than any earthly throng,
And sweeter is the thought of thee
Than any lovely song.

3 Thou hast put gladness in my heart;
Then well may I be glad!
Without the secret of thy love
I could not but be sad.

4 O Saviour, precious Saviour mine!
What will thy presence be, .
If such a life of joy can crown
Our walk on earth with thee?

## 128 Sheltered in the Rock.

1 SHELTERED in the Rock of Ages,
Kept from sin and all alarms,
The eternal God my refuge,
Safe in everlasting arms.
O how bulwarks pile around me;
Towers of strength and beauty shine,
Mighty fortress I have found thee,
Hid in God this soul of mine.

Cho.—Though the storms may surge around
I can sing while billows roll, [me;
For the mighty arms of Jesus
Clasp around my ransomed soul.

2 Blessed covert from the tempest,
Where secure my feet may stand;
Blessed Rock to give me shadow,
In a dry and weary land:
Though the foe may boast of shelter,
Yet their rock is not as ours;
Here the soul defies their legions,
Principalities and powers.

3 Covered in this Rock of Ages,
How the glory passes by,
Till, like Moses on the mountain,
God is seen by mortal eye;
Changed from glory unto glory,
Safe from storm and tempest shock,
Here I rest secure forever,
In this blessed rifted Rock.

# 129 The Unchanged Healer.

R. K. C.

"Himself took our infirmities and bore our sicknesses."
Matt. viii. 17.

R. Kelso Carter.

1. Jesus, thou ev-er art the same, To-day and yesterday are one; The glories
2. In thine own body on the tree My guilt and inbred sin were borne; My sickness-
3. Is thine arm shorten'd by the years? Thy promises outlaw'd by time? Canst thou not

**REFRAIN.**

of thy mighty name Forever mark God's risen Son. For me the Lord was cruci-
es were laid on thee, For me thy loving heart was torn.
see the suff'rer's tears That flow in ev'ry land and clime?

fied, For me he suffered, bled, and died: My Jesus bore it all for me,

*rit.*

My sin and sickness, on the tree.

4 Is anything too hard for thee?
  O God of all the earth, canst thou
  Give to my spirit liberty,
  But cannot heal my body now?

5 Away, my fears, I come to Christ,
  Soul, spirit, body, by thy word,
  Thro' thee, who once was sacrificed,
  Be wholly sanctified to God.

# 130                    Christ the Healer.                Tune above.

1 Tho' eighteen hundred years are past,
  Since thou didst in the flesh appear,
  Thy tender mercies ever last,
  And still thy healing power is here.

2 O Christ, thou art the Saviour still,
  In every place and age the same,
  Thou never hast forgot thy skill,
  Or lost the virtue of thy name.

3 Faith in thy changeless name I have,
  My good and kind Physician thou,
  From all disease thy hand can save,
  To perfect health restore me now.

4 All my disease, my every sin,
  To thee, O Jesus, I confess,
  Pardon my faults, my cure begin,
  And perfect me in holiness.

5 Be it according to thy Word,
  Accomplish now the work in me,
  And so shall I, with health restored,
  Devote my every power to thee.

## 131 Jesus, let Thy pitying eye.

1 JESUS, let thy pitying eye
　Call back a wandering sheep;
False to thee, like Peter, I
　Would fain, like Peter, weep.
Let me be by grace restored;
On me be all long suffering shown;
Turn, and look upon me, Lord,
And break my heart of stone.

2 Saviour, Prince, enthroned above,
　Repentance to impart,
Give me, through thy dying love,
　The humble, contrite heart:
Give what I have long implored,
A portion of thy grief unknown;
Turn, and look upon me, Lord,
And break my heart of stone.

3 See me, Saviour, from above,
　Nor suffer me to die;
Life, and happiness, and love
　Drop from thy gracious eye:
Speak the reconciling word,
And let thy mercy melt me down;
Turn, and look upon me, Lord,
And break my heart of stone.

4 Look, as when thy languid eye
　Was closed that we might live;
"Father," at the point to die
　My Saviour prayed,"forgive!"
Surely with thy dying word,　[done!"
He turns, and looks, and cries," 'Tis
O my bleeding, loving Lord,
Thou break'st my heart of stone!

## 132 Trusting Jesus, that is all.

1 SIMPLY trusting every day;
Trusting, though a stormy way;
Even when my faith is small,
Trusting Jesus, that is all.

Cho.—Trusting him while life shall last,
Trusting him till earth is past,—
Till within the jasper wall—
Trusting Jesus, that is all.

2 Brightly doth his Spirit shine
Into this poor heart of mine;
While he leads, I cannot fall,
Trusting Jesus, that is all.

3 Singing, if my way is clear;
Praying, if the path is drear;
If in danger, for him call—
Trusting Jesus, that is all.

4 Trusting as the moments fly,
Trusting as the days go by,
Trusting him, whate'er befall—
Trusting Jesus, that is all.

## 133 What Subdued.

1 WHAT subdued and conquered me?
Nothing but the blood of Jesus;
What first set my spirit free?
Nothing but the blood of Jesus.

Cho.—O precious is the flow
That makes me white as snow;
No other fount I know,
Nothing but the blood of Jesus.

2 What has sanctified my soul?
Nothing but the blood of Jesus;
What has made my spirit whole?
Nothing but the blood of Jesus.

3 What now saves me from all sin?
Nothing but the blood of Jesus;
What now keeps me pure within?
Nothing but the blood of Jesus.

4 O what joy now fills my soul!
Glory be to Jesus;
O how sweet the Lord's control!
Glory be to Jesus.

## 134 The Cross! the Cross!

1 THE cross! the cross! the blood-stained
The hallow'd cross I see,　[cross!
Reminding me of precious blood
That once was shed for me.

Cho.—Oh, the blood! the precious blood!
That Jesus shed for me
Upon the cross in crimson flood,
Just now by faith I see.

2 A thousand thousand fountains spring
Up from the throne of God;
But none to me such blessings bring,
As Jesus' precious blood.

3 That priceless blood my ransom paid
While I in bondage stood;
On Jesus all my sins were laid;
He saved me with his blood.

4 By faith that blood now sweeps away
My sins, as like a flood;
Nor lets one guilty blemish stay;
All praise to Jesus blood.

5 This wondrous theme will best employ
My harp before my God,
And make all heaven resound with joy,—
My Jesus crucified.

## 135 O for that Flame.

BATHURST.

Tune, SESSIONS.

1. O for that flame of living fire, Which shone so bright in saints of old;
Which bade their souls to heaven aspire,—Calm in distress, in danger bold.

2 Where is that Spirit, Lord, which dwelt
In Abrah'm's breast, and sealed him
   thine?   [melt.
Which made Paul's heart with sorrow
And glow with energy divine?—

3 That Spirit, which from age to age
Proclaimed thy love, and taught thy
Brightened Isaiah's vivid page, [ways?
And breathed in David's hallowed lays?

4 Is not thy grace as mighty now
As when Elijah felt its power;
When glory beamed from Moses' brow,
Or Job endured the trying hour?

5 Remember, Lord, the ancient days;
Renew thy work; thy grace restore;
And while to thee our hearts we raise,
On us thy Holy Spirit pour.

## 136 DAVIES. Lord, I am Thine. Tune, "Sessions."

1 LORD, I am thine, entirely thine,
Purchased and saved by blood divine;
With full consent thine would I be,
And own thy sov'reign right in me.

2 Thine would I live, thine would I die;
Be thine through all eternity;
The vow is past, beyond repeal,
And now I set the solemn seal.

3 Here, at that cross where flows the blood
That bought my guilty soul for God,
Thee, my new Master now I call,
And consecrate to thee my all.

4 Do thou assist a feeble worm
The great engagement to perform;
Thy grace can full assistance lend,
And on that grace I dare depend.

## 137 R. KELSO CARTER. Remember Me. Tune, "Lily Dale," Key Bb.

1 JESUS, for me thy blood was spilt
  Upon th'-accursed tree;  [guilt,
Redeem and cleanse my soul from
  O Lord, remember me.

Cho.—O Jesus, my Saviour!
  I look to thee;
Remember, Lord, thy dying groans,
  And then remember me.

2 Amid sin's dark and rushing flood
  I, desperate, cling to thee;

My only hope is Jesus' blood,
  My Lord, remember me.

3 Remember all my helplessness,
  And my infirmity;
Be thou my perfect righteousness,
  O Lord, remember me.

4 Deliver me from all my sin,
  And give full liberty;
Renew and cleanse without, within,—
  Dear Lord, remember me.

109

# 138    The Wondrous Cure.

JAMES NICHOLSON.      JNO. R. SWENEY.

1. When sick of in-bred sin, For health I vain-ly sought, Till
2. By works of righteous-ness, I tried in grace to grow; For
3. I could not touch his clothes; But I have touched his blood; And
4. O, what a wondrous cure Hath Jesus wrought in me! By

Je-sus Christ came in, And then the cure was wrought. O
one in my dis-tress The pro-gress was too slow; But
on my heart it flows, An ev-er-heal-ing flood. It
blood di-vine made pure; By power di-vine made free! The

wondrous power! O wondrous cure! Which makes my sinful nature pure.
faith in Christ, I now can say, I found to be the bet-ter way.
takes a-way the stains of sin; It cleanses me, and keeps me clean.
Ho-ly Ghost doth now control, And ful-ly sanc-ti-fy my soul.

**CHORUS.**

O grace divine! O wondrous love! Which brought my Saviour from above;

O wondrous power! O wondrous cure! Which makes my sinful nature pure.

# 139 The Story of Cleansing.

"BEULAH." GRACE WEISER.

1. 'Tis a sto-ry oft re-peat-ed, but it nev-er can grow old, The
2. How it rings thro' earth and heaven, sung by ransomed choirs above, Who
3. As I lis-ten to the message, how it thrills me with delight; The
4. Then why should I tarry long-er? Je-sus' call I will o-bey; I

5. Oh, this wonder-ful sal-vation, praise the dear Redeemer's name, It

story of the blood that makes us clean; 'Tis the sweetest story ears have heard or
by its power o'ercame and were made clean; How 'tis echoed by the pure of earth, sav'd
fountain now is o-pen, en-ter in; Whoso-ever will may venture in and
come, I wash, the promised rest I win, I will trust his power to keep me clean each

reaches me!—his praise I must begin; This my greatest joy, with all the saved for-

lips have ev-er told, The blood of Je-sus cleanseth from all sin.
by redeeming love; The blood of Je-sus cleanseth from all sin.
wash his garments white; The blood of Je-sus cleanseth from all sin.
moment, ev-'ry day; The blood of Je-sus cleanseth from all sin.

ev-er to proclaim, The blood of Je-sus cleanseth from all sin.

CHORUS.

A-ble to save to the uttermost, He of-fers us cleansing, and oh, it is free!

Wondrous salva-tion! it saves e-ven me! Washed in the blood of the Lamb.

111

From "Melodious Sonnets," by per.

# 140 Trust in thy Deliverer.

LAURA MILLER.                                                  JNO. R. SWENEY.

1. Go forth, O Christian sol - dier, Why shouldst thou fear to tread A
2. Be strong, O Christian sol - dier, And at thy post a - bide, Nor
3. Stand fast, O Christian sol - dier, Nor lay thy ar - mor down Till

path that bears the footprints Of him, thy living head; Take up thy cross with
heed the arrows fall - ing From foes on ev -'ry side; Let nothing daunt thy
thou by faith and patience Hast won the victor's crown; Then lift thy soul re-

firm - ness, Whate'er that cross may be, Remember him who car - ried A
cour - age, Whate'er the strife may be, But trust in thy Deliv - er - er, Who
joic - ing, And let thy glo-ry be In him, the Great Deliv - er - er, Who

CHORUS.

1. great - er one for thee. Trust in thy De - liv - er - er, Trust in thy De-
2, 3. shed his blood for thee.

liv - er-er, Oh, trust in thy De - liv - er - er, Who shed his blood for thee;

112

# Trust in thy Deliverer.—CONCLUDED.

Oh, trust in thy De - liv - er - er, Who shed his blood for thee.

## 141  Prisoners of Hope.

C. WESLEY.                                          R. KELSO CARTER.

1. { Prisoners of hope, lift up your heads, The day of liberty draws near!
{ Jesus, who on the serpent treads, Shall soon in your behalf ap - pear:

The Lord will to his temple come; Prepare your hearts to make him room.

2 Ye all shall find, whom in his word
    Himself hath caused to put your
  The Father of our dying Lord [trust,
    Is ever to his promise just;
  Faithful if we our sins confess,
  To cleanse from all unrighteousness.

3 O ye of fearful hearts, be strong! [up!
    Your downcast eyes and hands lift
  Ye shall not be forgotten long;
    Hope to the end, in Jesus hope!
  Tell him ye wait his grace to prove;
  And cannot fail if God is love.

## 142  All Things are Possible.

C. WESLEY.                                          Tune above.

1 ALL things are possible to him
    That can in Jesus' name believe;
  Lord, I no more thy truth blaspheme,
    Thy truth I lovingly receive;
  I can, I do believe in thee;
  All things are possible to me.

2 The most impossible of all
    Is that I e'er from sin should cease;
  Yet shall it be, I know it shall;
    Jesus, I trust thy faithfulness!
  If nothing is too hard for thee,
  All things are possible to me.

3 Thy mouth, O Lord, hath spoke, hath
        sworn,
    That I shall serve thee without fear,
  Shall find the pearl which others spurn,
    Holy, and pure, and perfect here;
  The servant as his Lord shall be;
  All things are possible to me

4 All things are possible to God,—
    To Christ, the power of God in man,-
  To me when I am all renewed,—
    When I in Christ am formed again,
  And witness from all sin set free,
  All things are possible to me.

## 143 Take my life and let it be.

FRANCIS RIDLEY HAVERGAL. Old English, arranged.

1. Take my life, and let it be Con - se - crat - ed, Lord, to thee;
2. Take my feet, and let them be Swift and beauti - ful for thee;

Take my hands and let them move At the im-pulse of thy love.
Take my voice, and let me sing Always, on - ly, for my King.

3 Take my lips and let them be
Filled with messages for thee;
Take my silver and my gold,—
Not a mite would I withhold.

4 Take my moments, and my days,
Let them flow in endless praise;
Take my intellect, and use
Every power as thou shalt choose.

5 Take my will, and make it thine;
It shall be no longer mine;
Take my heart,—it is thine own,—
It shall be thy royal throne.

6 Take my love,—my Lord, I pour
At thy feet its treasure-store!
Take myself, and I will be
Ever, only, all for thee!

## 144 The blood of Jesus cleanseth me.

The blood of Jesus cleanseth me, Cleanseth me, cleanseth me, The blood of Jesus

cleanseth me, Just now while I believe; Just now while I be - lieve, Just

now while I believe, The blood of Jesus cleanseth me, Just now while I believe.

## 145 Oh, how happy are they.

Oh, how happy, how happy are they, Oh, how happy, how happy are they, Oh, how

happy are they Who the Saviour obey, And have laid up their treasures above.

*[For other verses see opposite page.]*

146

## It is Good to be Here.

Rev. I. N. WILSON

JNO R. SWENEY, by per.

1. { While we bow in thy name, Oh, meet us a-gain, Fill our
   { May the Spir-it of grace, And the smiles of thy face, Gent-ly

D. S.—light streaming down makes the pathway all clear, It is

*Fine.* REFRAIN.

hearts with the light of thy love; } It is good to be here, it is
fall on us now from a-bove. }

good for us, Lord, to be here.

D. S.

good to be here, Thy perfect love now drives a-way all our fear, And

2 Our souls long for thee;
    Oh, may we now see
A sin-cleansing blood-wave appear;
    And feel, as it rolls
    In power o'er our souls,
It is good for us, Lord, to be here.

3 Thou art with us, we know;
    We feel the sweet flow          [tide;
Of the sin-cleansing wave's gladd'ning
    We are washed from our sin,
    Made all holy within,
And in Jesus we sweetly abide.

Copyright, 1879, by JNO. R. SWENEY.

DO RE MI FA SO LA SI

147          OH, HOW HAPPY ARE THEY.          Tune and Chorus above.

OH, how happy are they
    Who the Saviour obey,
And have laid up their treasures above;
    Tongue can never express
    The sweet comfort and peace
Of a soul in its earliest love.

2 That sweet comfort was mine,
    When the favor divine
I received thro' the blood of the Lamb;
    When my heart first believed,
    What a joy I received—
What a heaven in Jesus' name!

3 'Twas a heaven below
    My Redeemer to know,
And the angels could do nothing more
    Than to fall at his feet,
    And the story repeat,
And the Lover of sinners adore.

4 Jesus, all the day long,
    Was my joy and my song;
Oh, that all his salvation might see:
    He hath loved me, I cried,
    He hath suffered and died,
To redeem even rebels like me.

115

## 148     Love Divine.

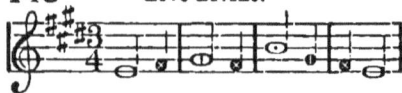

1 LOVE divine, all love excelling,
  Joy of heaven, to earth come down !
Fix in us thy humble dwelling;
  All thy faithful mercies crown.
Jesus, thou art all compassion,
  Pure, unbounded love thou art;
Visit us with thy salvation;
  Enter every trembling heart.

2 Breathe, O breathe thy loving Spirit
  Into every troubled breast !
Let us all in thee inherit,
  Let us find that second rest.
Take away our bent to sinning,
  Alpha and Omega be ;
End of faith, as its beginning,
  Set our hearts at liberty.

3 Come, almighty to deliver,
  Let us all thy life receive ;
Suddenly return, and never,
  Never more thy temples leave :
Thee we would be always blessing,
  Serve thee as thy hosts above,
Pray, and praise thee without ceasing,
  Glory in thy perfect love.

4 Finish then thy new creation ;
  Pure and spotless let us be ;
Let us see thy great salvation,
  Perfectly restored in thee :
Changed from glory into glory,
  Till in heaven we take our place,
Till we cast our crowns before thee,
  Lost in wonder, love, and praise.

## 149     There's a highway.

1 THERE'S a highway for the ransomed
  Where the children of the King,
Upon their pilgrim journey
  Triumphantly may sing,
Of a Saviour who redeemed them,
  And delivers from all sin,
His blood now makes me clean,

*Cho.*—Glory, glory, hallelujah ! :‖
  His blood now keeps me clean.

On the mountain tops of Beulah land,
  Or in the vale below,
Where temptations wildest hurricanes
  Their fiercest tempests blow,
In sorrow or in conflict now
  His grace he doth bestow,
His blood now makes me clean !

3 He that dwelleth in the covert
  Of the highest of the high,
Abides in perfect safety
  And the devil's hosts defies,
As 'neath Jehovah's mighty wings
  No evil can come nigh,
His blood now makes me clean.

4 As the past I can't live over,
  Nor insure the coming years,
I claim the now salvation—
  Nor live in future fears;
Cross no bridges till I reach them,
  And I shed no borrowed tears,
His blood now makes me clean.

## 150     Oh, how I love Jesus.

1 OH, how I love Jesus !
Oh, how I love Jesus !
Oh, how I love Jesus !
Because he first loved me.

2 How could I forget him ? :‖
Because he died for me.

3 I will live for Jesus, :‖
Who gave his life for me.

4 Blessed Jesus, keep me ! :‖
I trust alone in thee.

5 Glory be to Jesus !
Because he so loved me.

## 151     He is Calling.

1 THERE'S a wideness in God's mercy
Like the wideness of the sea :
There's a kindness in his justice
Which is more than liberty.

*Cho.*—He is calling "Come to me !"
Lord, I'll gladly haste to thee.

2 There is welcome for the sinner,
  And more graces for the good ;
There is mercy with the Saviour;
  There is healing in his blood.

3 For the love of God is broader
  Than the measure of man's mind
And the heart of the Eternal
  Is most wonderfully kind.

4 If our love were but more simple,
  We should take him at his word ;
And our lives would be all sunshine
  In the sweetness of our Lord.

## 152 The Blood-washed Pilgrim.

R. KELSO CARTER.

Arranged.

1. { I saw a blood-washed pilgrim, A sin - ner saved by grace,
Temp-ta-tions sore be - set him, But noth - ing could af - fright,

Up - on the king's great highway, With peaceful, shin - ing face. }
He said, "The yoke is ea - sy, The bur - den, it is light." }

**Chorus.**

Oh! palms of vic - to - ry, crowns of glo - ry, Palms of vic - to - ry I shall wear.

2.
His helmet was Salvation,
　A simple Faith his shield,
And Righteousness his breast-plate;
　The Spirit's sword he'd wield.
All fiery darts arrested,
　And quenched their blazing flight;
He cried, " The yoke is easy,
　The burden, it is light."—CHO.

3.
I saw him in the furnace,
　He doubted not, nor feared,
And in the flames beside him
　The Son of God appeared.
Though seven times 'twas heated
　With all the tempter's might,
He said, " The yoke is easy,
　The burden, it is light."—CHO.

4.
Mid storms, and clouds, and trials,
　In prison, at the stake,
He leaped for joy, rejoicing,
　'Twas all for Jesus' sake.
That God should count him worthy,
　Was such supreme delight,
He cried, " The yoke is easy,
　The burden, is so light."—CHO.

5.
I saw him overcoming,
　Through all the swelling strife,
Until he crossed the threshold
　Of God's Eternal Life.
The Crown, the Throne, the Sceptre,
　The Name, the Stone so White,
Were his, who found, in Jesus,
　The yoke and burden light.—CHO.

# 153

## Jesus Saves.

PRISCILLA J. OWENS.                                          WM. J. KIRKPATRICK.

1. We have heard a joy-ful sound, Je-sus saves, Je-sus saves;
2. Waft it on the roll-ing tide, Je-sus saves, Je-sus saves,
3. Sing a-bove the bat-tle's strife, Je-sus saves, Je-sus saves;
4. Give the winds a might-y voice, Je-sus saves, Je-sus saves,

Spread the glad-ness all a-round, Je-sus saves, Je-sus saves;
Tell to sin-ners, far and wide, Je-sus saves, Je-sus saves;
By his death and end-less life, Je-sus saves, Je-sus saves;
Let the na-tions now re-joice, Je-sus saves, Je-sus saves;

Bear the news to ev-'ry land, Climb the steeps and cross the waves,
Sing, ye is-lands of the sea, E-cho back, ye o-cean caves,
Sing it soft-ly thro' the gloom, When the heart for mer-cy craves,
Shout sal-va-tion full and free, High-est hills and deep-est caves,

Onward, 'tis our Lord's command, Je-sus saves, Je-sus saves.
Earth shall keep her ju-bi-lee, Je-sus saves, Je-sus saves.
Sing in tri-umph o'er the tomb, Je-sus saves, Je-sus saves.
This our song of vic-to-ry, Je-sus saves, Je-sus saves.

DO  RE  MI  FA  SO  LA  SI

# It Reaches Me.

MARY D. JAMES.

JNO. R. SWENEY.

1. Oh, this ut-ter-most sal-va-tion! 'Tis a fountain full and free,
2. How a-maz-ing God's compassion, That so vile a worm should prove
3. Je-sus, Saviour, I a-dore thee! Now thy love I will proclaim,

Pure, ex-haustless, ev-er flow-ing, Wondrous grace! it reaches me!
This stupend-ous bliss of Heav-en, This un-measured wealth of love!
I will tell the blessed sto-ry, I will mag-ni-fy thy name!

**CHORUS.**

It reaches me! it reaches me! Wondrous grace! it reaches me!

Pure, ex-haustless, ev-er flowing, Wondrous grace! it reaches me!

From "The Garner," by per.

119

DO RE MI FA SO LA SI

## 155 Cling, Brothers, Cling!

Rev. Henry Burton.                                    R Kelso Carter.

1. Cling, brothers, cling! Tho' waves and storms assail you, The Rock will never
2. Sing, brothers, sing! The sky is growing clear- er, The shores are coming
3. Pray, brothers, pray! The Saviour ev - er liv - eth, Himself his all he
4. Trust, brothers, trust! A - way with doubt and grieving, Believing is re-

fail you, O, cling, brothers, cling!
near - er, O, sing, brothers, sing!
giv - eth, O, pray, brothers, pray!
ceiv - ing, O, trust, brothers, trust!

5 Work, brothers, work!
The whitened fields are calling,
The evening shades are falling,
   O, work, brothers, work!

6 Watch, brothers, watch!
Look for the Lord's returning,
Let every lamp be burning,
   O, watch, brothers, watch!

## 156 He Watcheth Over me.

Lizzie Edwards                                    Jno. R. Sweney.

1. My heart with joy is bounding, My sky is calm and clear, Because my Lord and
2. He takes my hand so gently And guides my steps aright, He tunes my tongue with
3. Whene'er my thoughts are troubled, Or vexed with worldly care, I leave it all with
4. My faith in him grows brighter And stronger day by day; A constant joy be

CHORUS.

Saviour To me is drawing near. His prom - ise now I claim, His lov - ing
gladness And fills my soul with light.
   Jesus, And seek his aid in prayer.          His promise
gives me, That none can take away.                              His loving

120

## He Watcheth Over me.—CONCLUDED.

smile I see, And well I know where'er I go He watcheth o-ver me.

**157**

## Pure let me be.

R. KELSO CARTER.

Arranged with chorus by R. K. C.

1. Thro' the opened gates of glo-ry, Long time a - go, Jesus brought,—oh,
2. On the cross he died to save me, This, this I know; Full redemption
3. Jesus rose, while angels wondered, Long time a - go: Bars of death and

**CHORUS.**

wondrous story! Peace for our woe.  All the world is false and hollow;
then he gave me, Long time a - go.
hell he sundered, His love to show.

Pure let me be:   On - ly Je-sus I will follow; Lord, on - ly thee!

4 Jesus saves from sin and sinning,
　　Him I would know:
　Fought the fight and victory winning,
　　Long time ago.

5 Save me, cleanse me, keep me ever
　　White, white as snow;
　All was done,—I'll doubt it never,—
　　Long time ago.

121

## 158 Oh, 'tis Glory.

1 To thy cross, dear Christ, I'm clinging,
All my refuge and my plea;
Matchless is thy loving kindness,
Else it had not stooped to me.

*Cho.*—Oh, 'tis glory! oh, 'tis glory!
Oh, 'tis glory in my soul
For I've touched the hem of his garment,
And his power doth make me whole.

2 Long my heart hath heard thee calling,
But I thrust aside thy grace;
Yet, O boundless condescension!
Love is shining from thy face.

3 Love eternal, light eternal,
Close me safely, sweetly in;
Saviour, let thy balm of healing,
Ever keep me free from sin.

## 159 Thine All-victorious Love.

1 JESUS, thine all-victorious love
Shed in my heart abroad:
Then shall my feet no longer rove,
Rooted and fixed in God.

2 O, that in me the sacred fire
Might now begin to glow,
Burn up the dross of base desire,
And make the mountains flow!

3 O, that it now from heaven might fall,
And all my sins consume!
Come, Holy Ghost, for thee I call;
Spirit of burning, come!

4 Refining fire, go through my heart;
Illuminate my soul;
Scatter thy life through every part,
And sanctify the whole.

5 My steadfast soul, from falling free,
Shall then no longer move,
While Christ is all the world to me,
And all my heart is love.

## 160 I'll Live for Him.

1 MY life, my love I give to thee,
Thou Lamb of God, who died for me;
Oh, may I ever faithful be,
My Saviour and my God!

*Cho.*—I'll live for him who died for me,
How happy then my life shall be!
I'll live for him who died for me,
My Saviour and my God!

2 I now believe thou dost receive,
For thou hast died that I might live;
And now henceforth I'll trust in thee,
My Saviour and my God!

3 Oh, thou who died on Calvary,
To save my soul and make me free,
I consecrate my life to thee,
My Saviour and my God!

## 161 Glory to His Name.

1 DOWN at the cross where my Saviour died,
Down where for cleansing from sin I cried;
There to my heart was the blood applied;
Glory to his name.

*Cho.*— Glory to his name;:‖
There to my heart was the blood applied;
Glory to his name.

2 I am so wondrously saved from sin,
Jesus so sweetly abides within:
There at the cross where he took me in;
Glory to his name.

3 Oh, precious fountain, that saves from sin,
I am so glad I have entered in;
There Jesus saves me and keeps me clean,
Glory to his name.

4 Come to this fountain, so rich and sweet,
Cast thy poor soul at the Saviour's feet;
Plunge in to-day, and be made complete;
Glory to his name.

## 162 Sing of His Mighty Love.

1 OH, bliss of the purified, bliss of the free,
I plunge in the crimson tide opened for me;
O'er sin and uncleanness exulting I stand,
And point to the print of the nails in his hand.

*Cho.*—Oh, sing of his mighty love,
‖: Sing of his mighty love,:‖
Mighty to save.

2 Oh, bliss of the purified, Jesus is mine,
No longer in dread condemnation I pine;
In conscious salvation I sing of his grace,
Who lifteth upon me the light of his face.

3 Oh, bliss of the purified, bliss of the pure,
No wound hath the soul that his blood cannot cure;
No sorrow-bowed head but may sweetly find rest,
No tears but may dry them on Jesus' breast.

4 O Jesus the Crucified, thee will I sing,
My blessed Redeemer, my God and my King;
My soul filled with rapture shall shout o'er the grave,
And triumph in death in the "Mighty to Save."

## 163    The Altered Motto.

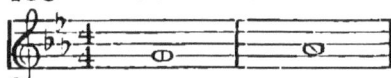

1 O THE bitter ‖ shame and sorrow, ‖
That a time could ‖ ever be, ‖
When I let the ‖ Saviour's pity ‖
Plead in ‖ vain and proudly answered,
All of self and none of thee.

2 Yet he found me, ‖ I beheld him ‖
Bleeding on the ac-‖cursed tree, ‖
Heard him pray, for-‖give them, Father, ‖
And my ‖ wistful heart said faintly,
Some of self and some of thee.

3 Day by day his ‖ tender mercy, ‖
Healing, helping. ‖ full and free, ‖
Sweet and strong, and, ‖ oh, so patient, ‖
Brought me ‖ lower while I whispered,
Less of self and more of thee.

4 Higher than the ‖ highest heaven, ‖
Deeper than the ‖ deepest sea, ‖
Lord, thy love ‖ at last has conquered, ‖
Grant me ‖ now my soul's desire,
None of self and all of thee,

## 164    The Land of Beulah.

1 I AM dwelling on the mountain,
Where the golden sunlight gleams
O'er a land whose wondrous beauty
Far exceeds my fondest dreams;
Where the air is pure ethereal,
Laden with the breath of flowers,
They are blooming by the fountain,
'Neath the amaranthine bowers.

Cho.—Is not this the land of Beulah,
Blessed, blessed land of light,
Where the flowers bloom forever,
And the sun is always bright.

2 I can see far down the mountain,
Where I wandered weary years,
Often hindered in my journey
By the ghosts of doubts and fears,
Broken vows and disappointments
Thickly sprinkled all the way,
But the Spirit led, unerring,
To the land I hold to-day.

3 I am drinking at the fountain,
Where I ever would abide;
For I've tasted life's pure river,
And my soul is satisfied;
There's no thirsting for life's pleasures,
Nor adorning, rich and gay,
For I've found a richer treasure,
One that fadeth not away.

## 165    Saved to the Uttermost.

1 SAVED to the uttermost: I am the Lord's,
Jesus my Saviour salvation affords,
Gives me his Spirit a witness within,
Whisp'ring of pardon, and saving from sin.

Cho.—Saved, saved, saved to the uttermost,
Saved, saved, by power divine;
Saved, saved, I'm saved to the uttermost,
Jesus the Saviour is mine.

2 Saved to the uttermost: Jesus is near,
Keeping me safely, he casteth out fear;
Trusting his promises, how I am blest,
Leaning upon him, how sweet is my rest.

3 Saved to the uttermost: this I can say,
"Once all was darkness, but now it is day,"
Beautiful visions of glory I see,
Jesus in brightness revealed unto me.

4 Saved to the uttermost: cheerfully sing
Loud hallelujahs to Jesus my King; [blood,
Ransomed and pardoned, redeemed by his
Cleansed from unrighteousness, glory to God.
—Wm. J. Kirkpatrick, by per.

## 166    All for Jesus!    Key Eb.

1 ALL for Jesus! all for Jesus!
All my being's ransomed powers;
All my thoughts and words and doings,
All my days and all my hours.
All for Jesus! all for Jesus!
All my days and all my hours.

2 Let my hands perform his bidding;
Let my feet run in his ways;
Let my eyes see Jesus only;
Let my lips speak forth his praise.
All for Jesus! all for Jesus!
Let my lips speak forth his praise.

3 Worldlings prize their gems of beauty,
Cling to gilded toys of dust,
Boast of wealth, and fame, and pleasure:
Only Jesus will I trust.
Only Jesus! only Jesus!
Only Jesus will I trust.

4 Since my eyes were fixed on Jesus,
I've lost sight of all beside,—
So enchained my spirit's vision,
Looking at the Crucified.
All for Jesus! all for Jesus!
All for Jesus crucified!

5 Oh, what wonder! how amazing!
Jesus, glorious King of kings,
Deigns to call me his beloved,
Lets me rest beneath his wings.
All for Jesus! all for Jesus!
Resting now beneath his wings.

# 167 We are More than Conquerors.

"Stand ye still, and see the salvation of the Lord." 2 Chr. xx. 17.

Mrs. FLORA B. HARRIS.

JNO. R. SWENEY.

1. What shall separate us From the love that bought us? Shall the pangs of anguish
2. Things to come or present, Whatsoe'er be- tide us,— Life nor death shall ever

Which the cross hath wrought us? Doubtings and distress- es, Fier- y tri- als
From our Lord di- vide us; Angels, powers, domin - ions, These shall fall be -

prove us; Yet am I per- suad - ed, None of these shall move us.
fore us; Clothed in his sal - va - tion, With his ban-ner o'er us.

CHORUS.

We are more than conquerors, More, yea, more; We are more than conquerors,
More, yea, more, more, yea, more,

More, yea, more; We are more than conquer- ors, We are more than
More, yea, more, more, yea, more;

124

DO RE MI FA SOL LA SI

con-quer-ors, We are more than conquer-ors, Thro' him that lov'd us.

3 Depths that are beneath us,
Heights that are above us,
Have no power to sunder,
Since he stooped to love us.

Prince of our Redemption,
Sons to glory bringing,
Thou hast made from sinners
Victors, crowned and singing.—*Cho.*

## 468 The Cleansing Blood.

CHAS. J. BUTLER.  Dr. H. L. GILMOUR.

1. Round Christ, the great incar - nate God, My arms of faith and love entwine;
2. Long sin's disease oppressed my soul,—The world could give no healing balm,—
3. A joy to unwashed souls unknown His cleansing blood has brought to me,
4. The vir - tue of my Saviour's blood To guil - ty souls I will proclaim,

*Fine.*

His blood, for ev' - ry sinner spilt, Now cleanseth this poor heart of mine.
But now the wondrous cure I've found, In Christ the sac - ri - fi - cial lamb.
And on my peaceful spir - it shines The light that beams from Cal - va - ry.
With joyful haste I'll spread abroad Je - sus the great Phy - si - cian's fame.

*D.S.*—I now have found the healing balm, In Calv'ry's precious, bleeding Lamb.

CHORUS. *D.S.*

Oh, yes, his blood, for sinners spilt, Now cleanseth me from sin and guilt;

125

DO RE MI FA SO LA SI

# O, Come, Come Away!

German Air, arr. by R. KELSO CARTER.

1. O, come, come a-way! for time's career is closing, Let worldly care hence-forth forbear, O, come, come a-way! Come, come our holy joys renew, Where love and heav'nly friendship grew, The Spirit welcomes you! O, come, come away!

2. A-wake ye, awake! no time now for reposing, "The Lord is near!" breaks on the ear, O, come, come away! Come, come where Jesus' love will be, Who says, "I'll meet with two or three," Sweet promise made to thee, O, come, come away!

3. Night soon will be o'er, and endless day appear-ing, Away from home no more we'll roam, O, come, come away! And when the trump of God shall sound The saints no more by Death are bound: He owns our Jesus crown'd; O, come, come away!

4. O, come, come a-way! my Saviour in thy glory. "Thy kingdom come, thy will be done;" O, come, come away! O, come, my Lord, thy right maintain, And take thy throne and on it reign; Then earth shall bloom again! O, come, come away!

Copyright, 1886, by JOHN J. HOOD.

## 170 C. WESLEY.    Arise, My Soul, Arise.    Tune above.

1 Arise, my soul, arise;
Shake off thy guilty fears;
The bleeding Sacrifice
In my behalf appears:
Before the throne my Surety stands,
My name is written on his hands.

2 He ever lives above,
For me to intercede;
His all-redeeming love,
His precious blood to plead;
His blood atoned for all our race,
And sprinkles now the throne of grace.

3 Five bleeding wounds he bears,
Received on Calvary;
They pour effectual prayers,

They strongly plead for me:
"Forgive him, O forgive," they cry,
"Nor let that ransomed sinner die."

4 The Father hears him pray,
His dear anointed One:
He cannot turn away
The presence of his Son:
His Spirit answers to the blood,
And tells me I am born of God.

5 My God is reconciled;
His pardoning voice I hear:
He owns me for his child;
I can no longer fear:
With confidence I now draw nigh,
And, "Father, Abba, Father," cry.

www.ingramcontent.com/pod-product-compliance
Lightning Source LLC
Chambersburg PA
CBHW030626270326
41927CB00007B/1326